ADVANCE PRAISE FOR

ZOMBIE POLITICS *and* CULTURE
in the Age of Casino Capitalism

"Henry A. Giroux is one of the foremost public intellectuals writing on issues of education in the U.S. today. This book is another testament to his long-standing quest for a just, egalitarian, and critical pedagogy against its distortion in the service of economic, political, and cultural power. His pungent style gives powerful voice to a passionate commitment to youth whose futures are placed in jeopardy by an educational system that marginalizes their intellectual, ethical, and emotional needs—and all too often becomes complicit in their criminalization. The book should be required reading for anyone concerned with the social consequences of the neoliberal assault on public education, which the present administration regretfully has done little to roll back."

—*Arif Dirlik, Liang Qichao Memorial Visiting Professor,*
Tsinghua University, Beijing

"Henry A. Giroux offers his most passionate defense yet of democracy and civic values in his new book. This volume is a must-read in dark times like these. Giroux has for decades been an outstanding tribune for democracy, an advocate for civic values and for questioning the unequal status quo. In this new book, he takes up more vigorously than ever the threats to the public sphere from reactionary forces gaining momentum. For Giroux, these threats to humane democracy fit the 'zombie aesthetic' now pervading television, film, and popular culture. Politics has become a monstrous caricature of public deliberation with wild propositions and charges spreading fear and division. Giroux explores the hostile forces sucking the blood out of our constitutional rights as well as the vitality out of ordinary families. We have become a society of monopolized wealth and distributed poverty, a culture of endless war, legalized torture, detention without trial, bursting prisons, and schools that turn our bright children into data. These intolerable conditions require the outrage and insight Giroux offers in his new book. He has written a volume inviting us to democratic action and civic restoration before these dark times grow even darker."

—*Ira Shor, Professor, City University of New York*

ZOMBIE POLITICS
and CULTURE
in the Age of Casino Capitalism

Toby Miller
General Editor

Vol. 23

PETER LANG
New York • Washington, D.C./Baltimore • Bern
Frankfurt • Berlin • Brussels • Vienna • Oxford

HENRY A. GIROUX

ZOMBIE POLITICS
and CULTURE
in the Age of Casino Capitalism

PETER LANG
New York • Washington, D.C./Baltimore • Bern
Frankfurt • Berlin • Brussels • Vienna • Oxford

Library of Congress Cataloging-in-Publication Data

Giroux, Henry A.
Zombie politics and culture in the age of casino capitalism /
Henry A. Giroux.
p. cm. — (Popular culture and everyday life; v. 23)
Includes bibliographical references and index.
1. United States—Social conditions—21st century.
2. United States—Social policy—21st century.
3. United States—Politics and government—2009–
4. Democracy—United States. 5. Capitalism—United States.
I. Title.
HN59.2.G56   306.0973'09051—dc22   2010041923
ISBN 978-1-4331-1227-0 (hardcover)
ISBN 978-1-4331-1226-3 (paperback)
ISSN 1529-2428

Bibliographic information published by **Die Deutsche Nationalbibliothek.**
Die Deutsche Nationalbibliothek lists this publication in the "Deutsche
Nationalbibliografie"; detailed bibliographic data is available
on the Internet at http://dnb.d-nb.de/.

Cover image by Gottfried Helnwein

The paper in this book meets the guidelines for permanence and durability
of the Committee on Production Guidelines for Book Longevity
of the Council of Library Resources.

© 2011 Peter Lang Publishing, Inc., New York
29 Broadway, 18th floor, New York, NY 10006
www.peterlang.com

Printed in the United States of America

For Susan

For Yoko Ono

Contents

SECTION II. ZOMBIE THEATER AND THE SPECTACLE OF ILLITERACY

SECTION III. BRUTALIZING YOUTH IN THE AGE OF ZOMBIE POLITICS

SECTION IV. CONCLUSION

Acknowledgments

This book would not have been written without the help of many friends who offered invaluable criticisms and support. I would like to especially thank Shirley Steinberg, David Clark, Ira Shor, Sophia McClennen, Christopher Robbins, Ken Saltman, Roger Simon, Stanley Aronowitz, Doug Morris, and Donaldo Macedo. I am grateful, once again, to Maya, Leslie, and Victoria at *Truthout* for providing me with the support and opportunity to publish many of these pieces. As always, Michael Peters has been a superb colleague and friend and has kindly published some of these pieces in *Policy Futures in Education*. Grace Pollock, my research assistant and colleague, has been of great assistance in reading and editing many of the articles in this book. Maya Sabados read many drafts, offered vital corrections, and as usual was an enormous help to me with every phase of the research. I also want to thank Chris Myers and Toby Miller for supporting this project. My graduate students, Jenny Fisher, Joe Frank, Tyler Pollard, and Sonya Zikíc, were terrific to work with and always provided insights in our many class discussions. My partner Susan Searls Giroux offered valuable suggestions on a number of articles and as usual made them much better. I also want to thank Dean Suzanne Crosta for her invaluable support and encouragement. And, while my canine companions Kaya and Miles did not read the manuscript, they helped in ways that only they can truly understand.

Introduction

Zombie Politics, Democracy, and the Threat of Authoritarianism

Education is the point at which we decide whether we love the world enough to assume responsibility for it and by the same token save it from ruin which, except for renewal, except for the coming of the new and young, would be inevitable. And education, too, is where we decide whether we love our children enough not to expel them from our world and leave them to their own devices, nor to strike from their hands their chance of undertaking something new, something unforeseen by us, but to prepare them in advance for the task of renewing a common world.

HANNAH ARENDT [1]

THE RISE OF ZOMBIE POLITICS

In the world of popular culture, zombies seem to be everywhere, as evidenced by the relentless slew of books, movies, video games, and comics. From the haunting *Night of the Living Dead* to the comic movie *Zombieland*, the figure of the zombie has captured and touched something unique in the contemporary imagination. But the dark and terrifying image of the zombie with missing body parts, oozing body fluids, and an appetite for fresh, living, human brains does more than feed the mass-marketing machines that prey on the spectacle of the violent, grotesque, and ethically comatose. There is more at work in this wave of fascination with the grotesquely walking hyper-dead than a Hollywood appropriation of the dark recesses and unrestrained urges of the human mind. The zombie phenomenon is now on display nightly on television alongside endless examples of destruction unfolding in real-time. Such a cultural fascination with proliferating images of the living hyper-dead and unrelenting human catastrophes that extend from a global economic meltdown to the earthquake in Haiti to the ecological disaster caused by the oil spill in the Gulf of Mexico signals a shift away from the hope that accompanies the living to a politics of cynicism and despair. The macabre double movement between "the dead that walk"[2] and those who are alive but are dying and suffering cannot be understood outside of the casino capitalism that now shapes every aspect of society in its own image. A casino capitalist zombie politics views competition as a form of social combat, celebrates war as an extension of politics, and legitimates a ruthless Social Darwinism in which particular individuals and groups are considered simply redundant, disposable—nothing more than human waste left to stew in their own misfortune—easy prey for the zombies who have a ravenous appetite for chaos and revel in apocalyptic visions filled with destruction, decay, abandoned houses, burned-out cars, gutted landscapes, and trashed gas stations.

The twenty-first-century zombies no longer emerge from the grave; they now inhabit the rich environs of Wall Street and roam the halls of the gilded monuments of greed such as Goldman Sachs. As an editorial in *The New York Times* points out, the new zombies of free-market fundamentalism turned "the financial system into a casino. Like gambling, the transactions mostly just shifted paper money around the globe. Unlike gambling, they packed an enormous capacity for collective and economic destruction—hobbling banks that made bad bets, freezing credit and economic activity. Society—not the bankers—bore the cost."[3] In this way, the zombie—the immoral, sub-Nietzschean, id-driven "other" who is "hyper-dead" but still alive as an avatar of death and cruelty—provides an apt metaphor for a new kind of authoritarianism that has a grip on contemporary politics in the United States.[4] This is an authoritarianism in which mindless self-gratification becomes the sanctioned norm and public issues collapse into the realm of privatized anger and rage. The rule of the market offers the hyper-dead an opportunity to exercise unprecedented power in American society, reconstructing civic and political culture almost entirely in the service of a politics that fuels the friend/enemy divide, even as democracy becomes the scandal of casino capitalism—its ultimate humiliation.

But the new zombies are not only wandering around in the banks, investment houses, and death chambers of high finance, they have an ever-increasing presence in the highest reaches of government and in the forefront of mainstream media. The growing numbers of zombies in the mainstream media have huge financial backing from the corporate elite and represent the new face of the culture of cruelty and hatred in the second Gilded Age. Any mention of the social state, putting limits on casino capitalism, and regulating corporate zombies puts Sarah Palin, Glenn Beck,

Rush Limbaugh, and other talking heads into a state of high rage. They disparage any discourse that embraces social justice, social responsibility, and human rights. Appealing to "real" American values such as family, God, and Guns, they are in the forefront of a zombie politics that opposes any legislation or policy designed to lessen human suffering and promote economic and social progress. As Arun Gupta points out, they are insistent in their opposition to "civil rights, school desegregation, women's rights, labor organizing, the minimum wage, Social Security, LGBT rights, welfare, immigrant rights, public education, reproductive rights, Medicare, [and] Medicaid."[5] The walking hyper-dead even oppose providing the extension of unemployment benefits to millions of Americans who are out of work, food, and hope. They spectacularize hatred and trade in lies and misinformation. They make populist appeals to the people while legitimating the power of the rich. They appeal to common sense as a way of devaluing a culture of questioning and critical exchange. Unrelenting in their role as archetypes of the hyper-dead, they are misanthropes trading in fear, hatred, and hyper-nationalism.

The human suffering produced by the walking hyper-dead can also be seen in the nativist apoplexy resulting in the racist anti-immigration laws passed in Arizona, the attempts to ban ethnic studies in public schools, the rise of the punishing state, the social dumping of millions of people of color into prisons, and the attempts of Tea Party fanatics and politicians who want to "take back America" from President Barack Obama—described in the new lexicon of right-wing political illiteracy as both an alleged socialist and the new Hitler. Newt Gingrich joins Glenn Beck and other members of the elite squad of the hyper-dead in arguing that Obama is just another version of Joseph Stalin. For Gingrich and the rest of the zombie ideologues, any discourse that advocates for social protections, easing human suffering, or imagining a better future is dismissed by being compared to the horrors of the Nazi holocaust. Dystopian discourse and End Times morbidity rule the collective consciousness of this group.

The "death panels" envisaged by Sarah Palin are not going to emerge from Obama's health care reform plan but from the toolkits the zombie politicians and talking heads open up every time they are given the opportunity to speak. The death threats, vandalism, and crowds shouting homophobic slurs at openly gay U.S. House Representative Barney Frank already speak to a fixation with images of death, violence, and war that now grips the country. Sarah Palin's infamous call to a gathering of her followers to "reload" in opposition to President Obama's policies—soon followed in a nationally televised press conference with a request for the American people to embrace Arizona's new xenophobic laws—makes her one of the most prominent of the political zombies. Not only has she made less-than-vague endorsements of violence in many of her public speeches, she has cheerfully embraced the new face of white supremacy in her recent unapologetic endorsement of racial profiling, stating in a widely reported speech that "It's time for Americans across this great country to stand up and say, 'We're all Arizonians now.'"[6] The current descent into racism, ignorance, corruption, and mob idiocy makes clear the degree to which politics has become a sport for zombies rather than engaged and thoughtful citizens.[7]

The hyper-dead celebrate talk radio haters such as Rush Limbaugh, whose fanaticism appears to pass without criticism in the mainstream media. Limbaugh echoes the fanatics who whipped up racial hatred in Weimar Germany, the ideological zombies who dissolved the line between reason and distortion-laden propaganda. How else to explain his claim "that environmentalist terrorists might have caused the ecological disaster in the gulf"?[8] The ethically frozen zombies that dominate screen culture believe that only an appeal to self-interest motivates people—a convenient counterpart to a culture of cruelty that rebukes, if not disdains, any appeal to the virtues of a moral and just society. They smile at their audiences while collapsing the distinction between opinions and reasoned arguments. They report on Tea Party rallies while feeding the misplaced ideological frenzy that motivates such gatherings but then refuse to comment on rallies all over the country that do not trade in violence or spectacle. They report uncritically on Islam bashers, such as the radical right-wing radio host Michael Savage, as if his ultra-extremist racist views are a legitimate part of the American mainstream. In the age of zombie politics, there is too little public outrage or informed public anger over the pushing of millions of people out of their homes and jobs, the defunding of schools, and the rising tide of homeless families and destitute communities. Instead of organized, massive protests against casino capitalism, the American public is treated to an endless and arrogant display of wealth, greed, and power. Armies of zombies tune in to gossip-laden entertainment, game, and reality TV shows, transfixed by the empty lure of celebrity culture.

The roaming hordes of celebrity zombie intellectuals work hard to fuel a sense of misguided fear and indignation toward democratic politics, the social state, and immigrants—all of which is spewed out in bitter words and comes terribly close to inciting violence. Zombies love death-dealing institutions, which accounts for why they rarely criticize the bloated military budget and the rise of the punishing state and its expanding prison system. They smile with patriotic glee, anxious to further the demands of empire as automated drones kill innocent civilians—conveniently dismissed as collateral damage—and the torture state rolls inexorably along in Afghanistan, Iraq, and in other hidden and unknown sites. The slaughter that inevitably follows catastrophe is not new, but the current politics of death has reached new heights and threatens to transform a weak democracy into a full-fledged authoritarian state.

A TURN TO THE DARK SIDE OF POLITICS

The American media, large segments of the public, and many educators widely believe that authoritarianism is alien to the political landscape of American society. Authoritarianism is generally associated with tyranny and governments that exercise power in violation of the rule of law. A commonly held perception of the American public is that authoritarianism is always elsewhere. It can be found in other allegedly "less developed/civilized countries," such as contemporary China or Iran, or it belongs to a fixed moment in modern history, often associated with the rise of twentieth-century totalitarianism in its different forms in Germany, Italy, and the Soviet Union under Stalin. Even as the United States became more disposed to modes of tyrannical power under the second Bush administration—demonstrated, for example, by the existence of secret CIA prisons, warrantless spying on Americans, and state-sanctioned kidnaping—mainstream liberals, intellectuals, journalists, and media pundits argued that any suggestion that the United States was becoming an authoritarian society was simply preposterous. For instance, the journalist James Traub repeated the dominant view that whatever problems the United States faced under the Bush administration had nothing to do with a growing authoritarianism or its more extreme form, totalitarianism.[9] On the contrary, according to this position, America was simply beholden to a temporary seizure of power by some extremists, who represented a form of political exceptionalism and an annoying growth on the body politic. In other words, as repugnant as many of Bush's domestic and foreign policies might have been, they neither threatened nor compromised in any substantial way America's claim to being a democratic society.

Against the notion that the Bush administration had pushed the United States close to the brink of authoritarianism, some pundits have argued that this dark moment in America's history, while uncharacteristic of a substantive democracy, had to be understood as temporary perversion of American law and democratic ideals that would end when George W. Bush concluded his second term in the White House. In this view, the regime of George W. Bush and its demonstrated contempt for democracy was explained away as the outgrowth of a random act of politics— a corrupt election and the bad-faith act of a conservative court in 2000 or a poorly run election campaign in 2004 by an uncinematic and boring Democratic candidate. According to this narrative, the Bush-Cheney regime exhibited such extreme modes of governance in its embrace of an imperial presidency, its violation of domestic and international laws, and its disdain for human rights and democratic values that it was hard to view such anti-democratic policies as part of a pervasive shift toward a hidden order of authoritarian politics, which historically has existed at the margins of American society. It would be difficult to label such a government other than as shockingly and uniquely extremist, given a political legacy that included the rise of the security and torture state; the creation of legal illegalities in which civil liberties were trampled; the launching of an unjust war in Iraq legitimated through official lies; the passing of legislative policies that drained the federal surplus by giving away more than a trillion dollars in tax cuts to the rich; the enactment of a shameful policy of preemptive war; the endorsement of an inflated military budget at the expense of much-needed social programs; the selling off of as many government functions as possible to corporate interests; the resurrection of an imperial presidency; an incessant attack against unions; support for a muzzled and increasingly corporate-controlled media; the government production of fake news reports to gain consent for regressive policies; the use of an Orwellian vocabulary for disguising monstrous acts such as torture ("enhanced interrogation techniques"); the furtherance of a racist campaign of legal harassment and incarceration of Arabs, Muslims, and immigrants; the advancement of a prison binge through a repressive policy of criminalization; the establishment of an unregulated and ultimately devastating form of casino capitalism; the arrogant celebration and support for the interests and values of big business at the expense of citizens and the common good; and the dismantling of social services and social safety nets as part of a larger campaign of ushering in the corporate state and the reign of finance capital?

AUTHORITARIANISM WITH A FRIENDLY FACE

In the minds of the American public, the dominant media, and the accommodating pundits and intellectuals, there is no sense of how authoritarianism in its soft and hard forms can manifest itself as anything other than horrible images of concentration camps, goose-stepping storm troopers, rigid modes of censorship, and chilling spectacles of extremist government repression and violence. That is, there is little understanding of how new modes of authoritarian ideology, policy, values, and social relations might manifest themselves in degrees and gradations so as to create the conditions for a distinctly undemocratic and increasingly cruel and oppressive social order. As the late Susan Sontag suggested in another context, there is a willful ignorance of how emerging registers of power and governance "dissolve politics into pathology."[10] It is generally believed that in a constitutional democracy, power is in the hands of the people, and that the long legacy of democratic ideals in America, however imperfect, is enough to prevent democracy from being subverted or lost. And yet the lessons of history provide clear examples of how the emergence of reactionary politics, the increasing power of the military, and the power of big business subverted democracy in Argentina, Chile, Germany, and Italy. In spite of these histories, there is no room in the public imagination to entertain what has become the unthinkable—that such an order in its contemporary form might be more nuanced, less theatrical, more cunning, less concerned with repressive modes of control than with manipulative modes of consent—what one might call a mode of authoritarianism with a distinctly American character.[11]

Historical conjunctures produce different forms of authoritarianism, though they all share a hatred for democracy, dissent, and civil liberties. It is too easy to believe in a simplistic binary logic that strictly categorizes a country as either authoritarian *or* democratic, which leaves no room for entertaining the possibility of a mixture of both systems. American politics today suggests a more updated if not a different form of authoritarianism. In this context, it is worth remembering what Huey Long said in response to the question of whether America could ever become fascist: "Yes, but we will call it anti-fascist."[12] Long's reply suggests that fascism is not an ideological apparatus frozen in a particular historical period but a complex and often shifting theoretical and political register for understanding how democracy can be subverted, if not destroyed, from within. This notion of soft or friendly fascism was articulated in 1985 in Bertram Gross's book *Friendly Fascism*, in which he argued that if fascism came to the United States it would not embody the same characteristics associated with fascist forms in the historical past. There would be no Nuremberg rallies, doctrines of racial superiority, government-sanctioned book burnings, death camps, genocidal purges, or the abrogation of the U.S. Constitution. In short, fascism would not take the form of an ideological grid from the past simply downloaded onto another country under different historical conditions. Gross believed that fascism was an ongoing danger and had the ability to become relevant under new conditions, taking on familiar forms of thought that resonate with nativist traditions, experiences, and political relations.[13] Similarly, in his *Anatomy of Fascism*, Robert O. Paxton argued that the texture of American fascism would not mimic traditional European forms but would be rooted in the language, symbols, and culture of everyday life. He writes: "No swastikas in an American fascism, but Stars and Stripes (or Stars and Bars) and Christian crosses. No fascist salute, but mass recitations of the Pledge of Allegiance. These symbols contain no whiff of fascism in themselves, of course, but an American fascism would transform them into obligatory litmus tests for detecting the internal enemy."[14] It is worth noting that Umberto Eco, in his discussion of "eternal fascism," also argued that any updated version of fascism would not openly assume the mantle of historical fascism; rather, new forms of authoritarianism would appropriate some of its elements, making it virtually unrecognizable from its traditional forms. Like Gross and Paxton, Eco contended that fascism, if it comes to America, will have a different guise, although it will be no less destructive of democracy. He wrote:

> Ur-Fascism [Eternal Fascism] is still around us, sometimes in plainclothes. It would be much easier for us if there appeared on the world scene somebody saying, "I want to reopen Auschwitz, I want the Blackshirts to parade again in the Italian squares." Life is not that simple. Ur-Fascism can come back under the most innocent of disguises. Our duty is to uncover it and to point our finger at any of its new instances—every day, in every part of the world.[15]

The renowned political theorist Sheldon Wolin, in *Democracy Incorporated*, updates these views and argues persuasively that the United States has produced its own unique form of authoritarianism, which he calls "inverted totalitarianism."[16] Wolin claims that under traditional forms of totalitarianism, there are usually founding texts such as *Mein Kampf*, rule by a personal demagogue such as Adolf Hitler, political change enacted by a revolutionary movement such as the Bolsheviks, the constitution rewritten or discarded, the political state's firm control over corporate interests, and an idealized and all-encompassing ideology used to create a unified and totalizing understanding of society. At the same time, the government uses all the power of its cultural and repressive state apparatuses to fashion followers in its own ideological image and collective identity.

In the United States, Wolin argues that an emerging authoritarianism appears to take on a very different form.[17] Instead of a charismatic leader, the government is now governed through the anonymous and largely remote hand of corporate power and finance capital. Political sovereignty is largely replaced by economic sovereignty as corporate power takes over the reins of governance. The dire consequence, as David Harvey points out, is that "raw money power wielded by the few undermines all semblances of democratic governance. The pharmaceutical companies, health insurance and hospital lobbies, for example, spent more than $133 million in the first three months of 2009 to make sure they got their way on health care reform in the United States."[18] The more money influences politics the more corrupt the political culture becomes. Under such circumstances, holding office is largely dependent on having huge amounts of capital at one's disposal, while laws and policies at all levels of government are mostly fashioned by lobbyists representing big business corporations and commanding financial institutions. Moreover, as the politics of health care reform indicate, such lobbying, as corrupt and unethical as it may be, is not carried out in the open and displayed by insurance and drug companies as a badge of honor—a kind of open testimonial to the disrespect for democratic governance and a celebration of their power. The subversion of democratic governance in the United States by corporate interests is captured succinctly by Chris Hedges in his observation that

> Corporations have 35,000 lobbyists in Washington and thousands more in state capitals that dole out corporate money to shape and write legislation. They use their political action com-

mittees to solicit employees and shareholders for donations to fund pliable candidates. The financial sector, for example, spent more than $5 billion on political campaigns, influenc[e] peddling and lobbying during the past decade, which resulted in sweeping deregulation, the gouging of consumers, our global financial meltdown and the subsequent looting of the U.S. Treasury. The Pharmaceutical Research and Manufacturers of America spent $26 million last year and drug companies such as Pfizer, Amgen and Eli Lilly kicked in tens of millions more to buy off the two parties. These corporations have made sure our so-called health reform bill will force us to buy their predatory and defective products. The oil and gas industry, the coal industry, defense contractors and telecommunications companies have thwarted the drive for sustainable energy and orchestrated the steady erosion of civil liberties. Politicians do corporate bidding and stage hollow acts of political theater to keep the fiction of the democratic state alive.[19]

Rather than being forced to adhere to a particular state ideology, the general public in the United States is largely depoliticized through the influence of corporations over schools, higher education, and other cultural apparatuses. The deadening of public values, civic consciousness, and critical citizenship is also the result of the work of anti-public intellectuals representing right-wing ideological and financial interests,[20] dominant media that are largely center-right, and a market-driven public pedagogy that reduces the obligations of citizenship to the endless consumption and discarding of commodities. In addition, a pedagogy of social and political amnesia works through celebrity culture and its counterpart in corporate-driven news, television, radio, and entertainment to produce a culture of stupidity, censorship, and diversionary spectacles.

DEPOLITICIZING FREEDOM AND AGENCY

Agency is now defined by a neoliberal concept of freedom, a notion that is largely organized according to the narrow notions of individual self-interest and limited to the freedom from constraints. Central to this concept is the freedom to pursue one's self-interests independently of larger social concerns. For individuals in a consumer society, this often means the freedom to shop, own guns, and define rights without regard to the consequences for others or the larger social order. When applied to economic institutions, this notion of freedom often translates into a call for removing government regulation over the market and economic institutions. This notion of a deregulated and privatized freedom is decoupled from the common good and any understanding of individual and social responsibility. It is an unlimited notion of freedom that both refuses to recognize the importance of social costs and social consequences and has no language for an ethic that calls us beyond ourselves, that engages our responsibility to others. Within this discourse of hyper-individualized freedom, individuals are not only "liberated from the constraints imposed by the dense network of social bonds," but are also "stripped of the protection which had been matter-of-factly offered in the past by that dense network of social bonds."[21]

Freedom exclusively tied to personal and political rights without also enabling access to economic resources becomes morally empty and politically dysfunctional. The much-heralded notion of choice associated with personal and political freedom is hardly assured when individuals lack the economic resources, knowledge, and social supports to make such choices and freedoms operative and meaningful. As Zygmunt Bauman points out, "The right to vote (and so, obliquely and at least in theory, the right to influence the composition of the ruler and the shape of the rules that bind the ruled) could be meaningfully exercised only by those 'who possess sufficient economic and cultural resources' to be 'safe from the voluntary or involuntary servitude that cuts off any possible autonomy of choice (and/or its delegation) at the root....[Choice] stripped of economic resources and political power hardly assure[s] personal freedoms to the *dispossessed*, who have no claim on the resources without which personal freedom can neither be won nor in practice enjoyed."[22] Paul Bigioni has argued that this flawed notion of freedom played a central role in the emerging fascist dictatorships of the early twentieth century. He writes:

> It was the liberals of that era who clamored for unfettered personal and economic freedom, no matter what the cost to society. Such untrammeled freedom is not suitable to civilized humans. It is the freedom of the jungle. In other words, the strong have more of it than the weak. It is a notion of freedom that is inherently violent, because it is enjoyed at the expense of others. Such a notion of freedom legitimizes each and every increase in the wealth and power of those who are already powerful, regardless of the misery that will be suffered by others as a result. The use of the state to limit such "freedom" was denounced by the laissez-faire liberals of the early 20th century. The use of the state to protect such "freedom" was fascism. Just as monopoly is the ruin of the free market, fascism is the ultimate degradation of liberal capitalism.[23]

This stripped-down notion of market-based freedom that now dominates American society cancels out any viable notion of individual and social agency. This market-driven notion of freedom emphasizes choice as an economic function defined largely as the right to buy things while at the same time cancelling out any active understanding of freedom and choice as the right to make rational choices concerning the very structure of power and governance in a society. In embracing a passive attitude toward freedom in which power is viewed as a necessary evil, a conservative notion of freedom reduces politics to the empty ritual of voting and is incapable of understanding freedom as a form of collective, productive power that enables "a notion of political agency and freedom that affirms the equal opportunity of all to exercise political power in order to participate in shaping the most important decisions affecting their lives."[24] This merging of the market-based understanding of freedom as the freedom to consume and the conservative-based view of freedom as a restriction from all constraints refuses to recognize that the conditions for substantive freedom do not lie in personal and political rights alone; on the contrary, real choices and freedom include the individual and collective ability to actively intervene in and shape both the nature of politics and the myriad forces bearing down on everyday life—a notion of freedom that can only be viable when social rights and economic resources are available to individuals. Of course, this notion of freedom and choice is often dismissed either as a vestige of socialism or simply drowned out in a culture that collapses all social considerations and notions of solidarity into the often cruel and swindle-based discourse of instant gratification and individual gain. Under such conditions, democracy is managed through the empty ritual of elections; citizens are largely rendered passive observers as a result of giving undue influence to corporate power in shaping all of the essential elements of political governance and decision making; and manufactured appeals to fear and personal safety legitimate both the suspension of civil liberties and the expanding powers of an imperial presidency and the policing functions of a militaristic state.

I believe that the formative culture necessary to create modes of education, thought, dialogue, critique, and critical agency—the necessary conditions of any aspiring democracy—is largely destroyed through the pacification of intellectuals and the elimination of public spheres capable of creating such a culture. Elements of a depoliticizing and commodifying culture become clear in the shameless propaganda produced by the so-called "embedded" journalists, while a corporate-dominated popular culture largely operates through multiple technologies, screen cultures, and video games that trade endlessly in images of violence, spectacles of consumption, and stultifying modes of (il)literacy. Funded by right-wing ideological, corporate, and militaristic interests, an army of anti-public intellectuals groomed in right-wing think tanks and foundations, such as the American Enterprise Institute and Manhattan Institute, dominate the traditional media, police the universities for any vestige of critical thought and dissent, and endlessly spread their message of privatization, deregulation, and commercialization, exercising a powerful influence in the dismantling of all public spheres not dominated by private and commodifying interests. These "experts in legitimation," to use Antonio Gramsci's prescient phrase, peddle civic ignorance just as they renounce any vestige of public accountability for big business, giant media conglomerates, and financial megacorporations. How else to explain that nearly twenty percent of the American people believe incorrectly that Obama is a Muslim!

Under the new authoritarianism, the corporate state and the punishing state merge as economics drives politics, and repression is increasingly used to contain all those individuals and groups caught in an expanding web of destabilizing inequality and powerlessness that touches everything from the need for basic health care, food, and shelter to the promise of a decent education. As the social state is hollowed out under pressure from free-market advocates, right-wing politicians, and conservative ideologues, the United States has increasingly turned its back on any semblance of social justice, civic responsibility, and democracy itself. This might explain the influential journalist Thomas Friedman's shameless endorsement of military adventurism in the *New York Times* article in which he argues that "The hidden hand of the market will never work without a hidden fist—McDonald's cannot flourish without McDonnell Douglas, the designer of the U.S. Air Force F-15. And the hidden fist that keeps the world safe for Silicon Valley's technologies to flourish is called the U.S. Army, Air Force, Navy and Marine Corps."[25] Freedom in this discourse is inextricably wedded to state and military violence and is a far cry from any semblance of a claim to democracy.

ZOMBIE POLITICS AND THE CULTURE OF CRUELTY

Another characteristic of an emerging authoritarianism in the United States is the correlation between the growing atomization of the individual and the rise of a culture of cruelty, a type of zombie politics in which the living dead engage in forms of rapacious behavior that destroy almost every facet of a substantive democratic polity. There is a mode of terror rooted in a neoliberal market-driven society that numbs many people just as it wipes out the creative faculties of imagination, memory, and critical thought. Under a regime of privatized utopias, hyper-individualism, and ego-centered values, human beings slip into a kind of ethical somnolence, indifferent to the plight and suffering of others. Though writing in a different context, the late Frankfurt School theorist Leo Lowenthal captured this mode of terror in his comments on the deeply sedimented elements of authoritarianism rooted in modern civilization. He wrote:

> In a system that reduces life to a chain of disconnected reactions to shock, personal communication tends to lose all meaning....The individual under terrorist conditions is never alone and always alone. He becomes numb and rigid not only in relation to his neighbor but also in relation to himself; fear robs him of the power of spontaneous emotional or mental reaction. Thinking becomes a stupid crime; it endangers his life. The inevitable consequence is that stupidity spreads as a contagious disease among the terrorized population. Human beings live in a state of stupor, in a moral coma.[26]

Implicit in Lowenthal's commentary is the assumption that as democracy becomes a fiction, the moral mechanisms of language, meaning, and ethics collapse, and a cruel indifference takes over diverse modes of communication and exchange, often as a register of the current paucity of democratic values, identities, and social relations. Surely, this is obvious today as all vestiges of the social compact, social responsibility, and modes of solidarity give way to a form of Social Darwinism with its emphasis on ruthlessness, cruelty, war, violence, hyper modes of masculinity, and a disdain for those considered weak, dependent, alien, or economically unproductive. A poverty of civic ideals is matched not only by a poverty of critical agency but also by the disappearance among the public of the importance of moral and social responsibilities. As public life is commercialized and commodified, the pathology of individual entitlement and narcissism erodes those public spaces in which the conditions for conscience, decency, self-respect, and dignity take root. The delusion of endless growth coupled with an "obsession with wealth creation, the cult of privatization [and] uncritical admiration for unfettered markets, and disdain for the public sector" has produced a culture that seems "consumed by locusts" in "an age of pygmies."[27]

This culture of cruelty is especially evident in the hardships and deprivations now visited upon many young people in the United States. We have 13.3 million homeless children; one child in five lives in poverty; too many are now under the supervision of the criminal justice system, and many more young adults are unemployed and lack any hope for the future.[28] Moreover, we are subjecting more and more children to psychiatric drugs as a way of controlling their alleged unruly behavior while providing huge profits for drug companies. As Evelyn Pringle points out, "in 2006 more money was spent on treating mental disorders in children aged 0 to 17 than for any other medical condition, with a total of $8.9 billion."[29] Needless to say, the drugging of American children is less about treating genuine mental disorders than it is about punishing so-called unruly children, largely children of the poor, while creating "lifelong patients and repeat customers for Pharma!"[30] Stories abound about poor young people being raped, beaten, and dying in juvenile detention centers, needlessly trafficked into the criminal justice system as part of a profit-making scheme cooked up by corrupt judges and private correction facilities administrators, and being given powerful antipsychotic medicines in schools and other state facilities.[31] Unfortunately, this regression to sheer Economic Darwinism is not only evident in increasing violence against young people, cutthroat reality TV shows, hate radio, and the Internet, it is also on full display in the discourse of government officials and politicians and serves as a register of the prominence of both a kind of political infantilism and a culture of cruelty. For instance, the Secretary of Education, Arne Duncan, recently stated in an interview in February 2010 that "the best thing that happened to the education system in New Orleans was Hurricane Katrina."[32] Duncan's point, beyond the incredible inhumanity reflected in such a comment, was that it took a disaster that uprooted thousands of individuals and families and caused enormous amounts of suffering to enable the Obama administration to implement a massive educational system pushing charter schools based on market-driven principles that disdain public val-

ues, if not public schooling itself. This is the language of cruelty and zombie politicians, a language indifferent to the ways in which people who suffer great tragedies
are expelled from their histories, narratives, and right to be human. Horrible
tragedies caused in part by government indifference are now covered up in the discourse and ideals inspired by the logic of the market. This mean and merciless streak
was also on display recently when Lieutenant Governor Andre Bauer, who is running for the Republican nomination for governor in South Carolina, stated that giving people government assistance was comparable to "feeding stray animals." The
utterly derogatory and implicitly racist nature of his remark became obvious in the
statement that followed: "You know why? Because they breed. You're facilitating the
problem if you give an animal or a person ample food supply. They will reproduce,
especially ones that don't think too much further than that. And so what you've got
to do is you've got to curtail that type of behavior. They don't know any better."[33]

Lowenthal's argument that in an authoritarian society "stupidity spreads as a
contagious disease" is evident in a statement made by Michele Bachmann, a
Republican congresswoman, who recently argued that "Americans should purchase
[health] insurance with their own tax-free money."[34] That 43 million Americans
are without health insurance because they cannot afford it seems lost on Bachmann,
whose comments suggest that these uninsured individuals, families, unemployed
workers, and children are not simply a disposable surplus but actually invisible and
therefore unworthy of any acknowledgment.

The regressive politics and moral stupidity are also evident in the emergence
of right-wing extremists now taking over the Republican Party. This new and
aggressive political formation calls for decoupling market-driven financial institutions from any vestige of political and governmental constraint, celebrates emotion
over reason, treats critical intelligence as a toxin possessed largely by elites, wraps
its sophomoric misrepresentations in an air of beyond-interrogation "we're just
folks" insularity, and calls for the restoration of a traditional, white, Christian,
male-dominated America.[35] Such calls embody elements of a racial panic that are
evident in all authoritarian movements and have increasingly become a defining feature of a Republican Party that has sided with far-right-wing thugs and goon
squads intent on disrupting any vestige of the democratic process. This emerging
authoritarian element in American political culture is embodied in the wildly popular media presence of Rush Limbaugh and Glenn Beck—right-wing extremists
who share a contempt for reason and believe in organizing politics on the model of
war, unconditional surrender, personal insults, hyper-masculine spectacles, and the
complete destruction of one's opponent.

The culture of cruelty, violence, and slander was on full display as the Obama
administration successfully passed a weak version of health care reform in 2010.
Stoked by a Republican Party that has either looked away or in some cases support-

ed the coded language of racism and violence, it was no surprise that there was bare-ly a peep out of Republican Party leaders when racial and homophobic slurs were hurled by Tea Party demonstrators at civil rights legend Jon Lewis and openly gay Barney Frank, both firm supporters of the Obama health policies. Even worse is the nod to trigger-happy right-wing advocates of violence that conservatives such as Sarah Palin have suggested in their response to the passage of the health care bill. For instance, Frank Rich argues that

> this bill that inspired G.O.P. congressmen on the House floor to egg on disruptive protest-ers even as they were being evicted from the gallery by the Capitol Police last Sunday. It's this bill that prompted a congressman to shout "baby killer" at Bart Stupak, a staunch anti-abortion Democrat. It's this bill that drove a demonstrator to spit on Emanuel Cleaver, a black representative from Missouri. And it's this "middle-of-the-road" bill, as Obama accurately calls it, that has incited an unglued firestorm of homicidal rhetoric, from "Kill the bill!" to Sarah Palin's cry for her followers to "reload." At least four of the House members hit with death threats or vandalism are among the 20 political targets Palin marks with rifle crosshairs on a map on her Facebook page.[36]

There is more at work here than the usual right-wing promotion of bigotry and ignorance; there is the use of violent rhetoric and imagery that mimics the discourse of terrorism reminiscent of Oklahoma bomber Timothy McVeigh, dangerous right-wing militia groups, and other American-style fascists. As Chris Hedges insists, "The language of violence always presages violence"[37] and fuels an authoritarian-ism that feeds on such excesses and the moral coma that accompanies the inabili-ty of a society to both question itself and imagine an alternative democratic order. How else can one read the "homicidal rhetoric" that is growing in America as any-thing other than an obituary for dialogue, democratic values, and civic courage? What does it mean for a democracy when the general public either supports or is silent in the face of widely publicized events such as black and gay members of Congress being subjected to racist and homophobic taunts, a black congressman being spit on, and the throwing of bricks through the office windows of some leg-islators who supported the health care bill? What does it mean for a democracy when there is little collective outrage when Sarah Palin, a leading voice in the Republican Party, mimics the tactics of vigilantes by posting a map with crosshairs on the districts of Democrats and urges her supporters on with the shameful slo-gan "Don't Retreat. Instead—RELOAD!" Under such circumstances, the brandish-ing of assault weapons at right-wing political rallies, the posters and signs comparing Obama to Hitler, and the ever-increasing chants to "Take Our Country Back" echoes what Frank Rich calls a "small-scale mimicry of Kristallnacht."[38] Violence and aggression are now openly tolerated and in some cases promoted. The chants, insults, violence, and mob hysteria all portend a dark period in American history—

an historical conjuncture in the death knell for democracy is being written as the media turn such events into spectacles rather than treat them as morally and politically repugnant acts more akin to the legacy of fascism than the ideals of an aspiring democracy. All the while the public yawns or, more troubling, engages fantasies of reloading.

Unfortunately, the problems now facing the United States are legion and further the erosion of a civic and democratic culture. Some of the most glaring issues are massive unemployment; a rotting infrastructure; the erosion of vital public services; the dismantling of the social safety net; expanding levels of poverty, especially for children; and an imprisonment binge largely affecting poor minorities of color. But such a list barely scratches the surface. In addition, we have witnessed in the last thirty years the restructuring of public education as either a source of profit for corporations or an updated version of control modeled after prison culture coupled with an increasing culture of lying, cruelty, and corruption, all of which belie a democratic vision of America that now seems imaginable only as a nostalgic rendering of the founding ideals of democracy.

DANGEROUS AUTHORITARIANISM OR SHRINKING DEMOCRACY?

Needless to say, many would disagree with Wolin's view that the United States is in the grip of a new and dangerous authoritarianism that makes a mockery of the country's moral claim to being a model of democracy at home and for the rest of the world. For instance, liberal critic Robert Reich, the former Secretary of Labor under President Bill Clinton, refers to America's changing political landscape as a "shrinking democracy."[39] For Reich, democracy necessitates three things: "(1) Important decisions are made in the open. (2) The public and its representatives have an opportunity to debate them, so the decisions can be revised in light of what the public discovers and wants. And (3) those who make the big decisions are accountable to voters."[40] If we apply Reich's notion of democracy, then it becomes evident that the use of the term democracy is neither theoretically apt nor politically feasible at the current historical moment as a description of the United States. All of the conditions he claims are crucial for a democracy are now undermined by financial and economic interests that control elections, buy off political representatives, and eliminate those public spheres where real dialogue and debate can take place. It is difficult to imagine that anyone looking at a society in which an ultra-rich financial elite and megacorporations have the power to control almost every aspect of politics—from who gets elected to how laws are enacted—could possibly mistake this social order and system of government for a democracy. A more appropriate understanding of democracy comes from Wolin in his claim that democracy is about the conditions that make it possible for ordinary people to better their lives by becoming political beings and by making power responsive to their hopes and needs. What is at stake in democratic politics is whether ordinary men and women can recognize that their concerns are best protected and cultivated under a regime whose actions are governed by principles of commonality, equality, and fairness, a regime in which taking part in politics becomes a way of staking out and sharing in a common life and its forms of self-fulfillment. Democracy is not about bowling together but about managing together those powers that immediately and significantly affect the lives and circumstances of others and one's self. Exercising power can be humbling when the consequences are palpable rather than statistical—and rather different from wielding power at a distance, at, say, an "undisclosed bunker somewhere in northern Virginia."[41]

Wolin ties democracy not merely to participation and accountability but to the importance of the formative culture necessary for critical citizens and the need for a redistribution of power and wealth, that is, a democracy in which power is exercised not just for the people by elites but by the people in their own collective interests. But more importantly, Wolin and others recognize that the rituals of voting and accountability have become empty in a country that has been reduced to a lockdown universe in which torture, abuse, and the suspension of civil liberties have become so normalized that more than half of all Americans now support the use of torture under some circumstances.[42] Torture, kidnapping, indefinite detention, murder, and disappeared "enemy combatants" are typical practices carried out in dictatorships, not in democracies, especially in a democracy that allegedly has a liberal president whose election campaign ran on the promise of change and hope. Maybe it's time to use a different language to name and resist the registers of power and ideology that now dominate American society.

While precise accounts of the meaning of authoritarianism, especially fascism, abound, I have no desire, given its shifting nature, to impose a rigid or universal definition. What is to be noted is that many scholars, such as Kevin Passmore and Robert O. Paxton, agree that authoritarianism is a mass movement that emerges out of a failed democracy, and its ideology is extremely anti-liberal, anti-democratic, and anti-socialistic.[43] As a social order, it is generally characterized by a system of terror directed against perceived enemies of the state; a monopolistic control of the mass media; an expanding prison system; a state monopoly of weapons; political rule by privileged groups and classes; control of the economy by a limited number of people; unbridled corporatism; "the appeal to emotion and myth rather than reason; the glorification of violence on behalf of a national cause; the mobilization and militarization of civil society; [and] an expansionist foreign policy intended to promote national greatness."[44] All of these tendencies were highly visible during the former Bush administration. With the election of Barack Obama to the presidency, there was a widespread feeling among large sections of the American public and its intellectuals that the threat of authoritarianism had passed. And yet there are many troubling signs that in spite of the election of Obama, authoritarian policies not only continue to unfold unabated within his administration but continue outside of his power to control them. In this case, antidemocratic forces seem to align with many of the conditions that make up what Wolin calls the politics of inverted totalitarianism.

I think it is fair to say that authoritarianism can permeate the lived relations of a political culture and social order and can be seen in the ways in which such relations exacerbate the material conditions of inequality, undercut a sense of individual and social agency, hijack democratic values, and promote a deep sense of hopelessness, cynicism, and eventually unbridled anger. This deep sense of cynicism and despair on the part of the polity in the face of unaccountable corporate and political power lends credence to Hannah Arendt's notion that at the heart of totalitarianism is the disappearance of the thinking, dialogue, and speaking citizens who make politics possible. Authoritarianism as both an ideology and a set of social practices emerges within the lives of those marked by such relations, as its proponents scorn the present while calling for a revolution that rescues a deeply anti-modernist past in order to revolutionize the future.

Determining for certain whether we are in the midst of a new authoritarianism under the leadership of Barack Obama is difficult, but one thing is clear: any new form of authoritarianism that emerges in the current time will be much more powerful and complex in its beliefs, mechanisms of power, and modes of control than the alleged idealism of one man or one administration. The popular belief, especially after McCain's defeat, was that the country had made a break with its morally transgressive and reactionary past and that Obama signified not just hope but political redemption. Such views ignored both the systemic and powerfully organized financial and economic forces at work in American society while vastly overestimating the power of any one individual or isolated group to challenge and transform them. Even as the current economic meltdown revealed the destructive and distinctive class character of the financial crisis, the idea that the crisis was rooted in systemic causes that far exceeded a few bailouts was lost even on liberal economists such as Paul Krugman, Jeffrey Sachs, and Joseph Stiglitz.

Within such economic analyses and narratives of political redemption, the primacy of hope and "critical exuberance" took precedence over the reality of established corporate power, ideological interests, and the influence of the military-industrial complex. As Judith Butler warned soon after Obama's victory, "Obama is, after all, hardly a leftist, regardless of the attributions of 'socialism' proffered by his conservative opponents. In what ways will his actions be constrained by party politics, economic interests, and state power; in what ways have they been compromised already? If we seek through this presidency to overcome a sense of dissonance, then we will have jettisoned critical politics in favor of an exuberance whose phantasmatic dimensions will prove consequential."[45] In retrospect, Butler's comments have proven prescient, and the hope that accompanied Obama's election has now been tempered by not simply despair but in many quarters outright and legitimate anger.

If Bush's presidency represented an exceptional anti-democratic moment, it would seem logical that the Obama administration would have examined, condemned, and dismantled policies and practices at odds with the ideals of an aspiring democracy. Unfortunately, such has not been the case under Obama, at least up to this point in his administration. Within the past few years, Obama has moved decidedly to the right, and in doing so has extended some of the worst elements of the counter-terrorism policies of the Bush administration. He has endorsed the use of military commissions, argued for the use of indefinite detention with no charges or legal recourse for Afghan prisoners, extended the USA Patriot Act,[46] continued two wars while expanding the war in Afghanistan, and largely reproduced Bush's market-driven approach to school reform.[47] As Noam Chomsky points out, Obama has done nothing to alter the power and triumph of financial liberalization in the past thirty years.[48] He bailed out banks and financial investment institutions at the expense of the 26.3 million Americans who are either unemployed or do not have full-time jobs along with the millions who have lost their homes. His chief economic and foreign policy advisors—Tim Geithner, Lawrence Summers, and Robert Gates—represent a continuation of a military and big business orientation that is central to the ideologies and power relations of a undemocratic and increasingly bankrupt economic and political system. While claiming to enact policies designed to reduce the federal deficit, Obama plans to cut many crucial domestic programs while increasing military spending, the intelligence budget, and foreign military aid. Obama has requested a defense budget for 2011 of $708 billion, in addition to calling for $33 billion to finance the wars in Iraq and Afghanistan. This budget is almost as large as the rest of the entire world's defense spending combined. Roger Hodge provides a useful summary of Obama's failings, extending from the perversion of the rule of law to the authoritarian claim of "sovereign immunity." He writes:

> Obama promised to end the war in Iraq, end torture, close Guantánamo, restore the constitution, heal our wounds, and wash our feet. None of these things has come to pass. As president, with few exceptions, Obama either has embraced the unconstitutional war powers claimed by his predecessor or has left the door open for their quiet adoption at some later date. Leon Panetta, director of the Central Intelligence Agency, has declared that the right to kidnap (known as "extraordinary rendition") foreigners will continue, just as the Bush administration's expansive doctrine of state secrets continues to be used in court against those wrongfully detained and tortured by our security forces and allies. Obama has adopted military commissions, once an unpardonable offense against our best traditions, to prosecute terrorism cases in which legitimate convictions cannot be obtained....The principle of habeas corpus, sacred to candidate Obama as "the essence of who we are," no longer seems so essen-

tial, and reports continue to surface of secret prisons hidden from due process and the Red Cross. Waterboarding has been banned, but other "soft" forms of torture, such as sleep deprivation and force-feeding, continue—as do the practices, which once seemed so terribly important to opponents of the Bush regime, of presidential signing statements and warrantless surveillance. In at least one respect, the Obama Justice Department has produced an innovation: a claim of "sovereign immunity" in response to a lawsuit seeking damages for illegal spying. Not even the minions of George W. Bush, with their fanciful notions of the unitary executive, made use of this constitutionally suspect doctrine, derived from the ancient common-law assumption that "the King can do no wrong," to defend their clear violations of the federal surveillance statute.[49]

Moreover, by giving corporations and unions unlimited freedom to contribute to elections, the recent Supreme Court decision in *Citizens United* v. *Federal Election Commission* provided a final step in placing the control of politics more firmly in the hands of big money and large corporations. In this ruling, democracy—like everything else in American culture—was treated as a commodity and offered up to the highest bidder. As a result, whatever government regulations are imposed on big business and the financial sectors will be largely ineffective and will do little to disrupt casino capitalism's freedom from political, economic, and ethical constraints. Chris Hedges is right in insisting that the Supreme Court's decision "carried out a coup d'état in slow motion. The coup is over. We lost. The ruling is one more judicial effort to streamline mechanisms for corporate control. It exposes the myth of a functioning democracy and the triumph of corporate power....The corporate state is firmly cemented in place."[50]

In light of his conservative, if not authoritarian, policies, Obama's once-inspiring call for hope has been reduced to what appears to be simply an empty performance, one that "favours the grand symbolic gesture over deep structural change every time."[51] What once appeared as inspired rhetoric has largely been reduced to fodder for late-night television comics, while for a growing army of angry voters it has become nothing more than a cheap marketing campaign and disingenuous diversion in support of moneyed interests and power. Obama's rhetoric of hope is largely contradicted by policies that continue to reproduce a world of egotistic self-referentiality, an insensitivity to human suffering, massive investments in military power, and an embrace of those market-driven values that produce enormous inequalities in wealth, income, and security. There is more at stake here than a politics of misrepresentation and bad faith. There is an invisible register of politics that goes far beyond the contradiction between Obama's discourse and his right-wing policies. What we must take seriously in Obama's policies is the absence of anything that might suggest a fundamental power shift away from casino capitalism to policies that would develop the conditions "that make it possible for ordinary people to better their lives by becoming political beings and by making power responsive to their hopes and needs."[52] In Obama's world, cutthroat competition is still the name of the game, and individual choice is still simply about a hunt for bargains. Lost here is any notion of political and social responsibility for the welfare, autonomy, and dignity of all human beings but especially those who are marginalized because they lack food, shelter, jobs, and other crucial basic needs. But then again, this is not Obama's world; it is a political order and mode of economic sovereignty that has been in the making for quite some time and now shapes practically every aspect of culture, politics, and civic life. In doing so it has largely destroyed any vestige of real democracy in the United States.

I am not suggesting that in light of Obama's continuation of some of the deeply structured authoritarian tendencies in American society that people should turn away from the language of hope, but I am saying that they should avoid a notion of hope that is as empty as it is disingenuous. What is needed is a language of critique and hope that mutually inform each other, and engagement in a discourse of hope that is concretely rooted in real struggles and capable of inspiring a new political language and collective vision among a highly conservative and fractured polity. Maybe it is time to shift the critique of Obama away from an exclusive focus on the policies and practices of his administration and develop a new language, one with a longer historical purview and deeper understanding of the ominous forces that now threaten any credible notion of the United States as an aspiring democracy. As Stuart Hall insists, we "need to change the scale of magnification" in order to make visible the anti-democratic relations often buried beneath the hidden order of politics that have taken hold in the United States in the last few decades.[53] It may be time to shift the discourse away from focusing on either Obama's failures or urging progressives and others to develop "the organizational power to make muscular demands"[54] on the Obama administration. Maybe the time has come to focus on the ongoing repressive and systemic conditions, institutions, ideologies, and values that have been developing in American society for the last thirty years, forces that are giving rise to a unique form of American authoritarianism. I agree with Sheldon Wolin that the "fixation upon" Obama now "obscures the problems" we are facing.[55] Maybe it is time to imagine what democracy would look like outside of what we have come to call capitalism, not simply neoliberalism at its most extreme manifestation. Maybe it is time to fight for the formative culture and modes of thought and agency that are the very foundations of democracy. And maybe it is time to mobilize a militant, far-reaching social movement to challenge the false claims that equate democracy and capitalism.

If it is true that a new form of authoritarianism is developing in the United States, undercutting any vestige of a democratic society, then it is equally true that there is nothing inevitable about this growing threat. The long and tightening grip of authoritarianism in American political culture can be resisted and transformed. This dystopic future will not happen if intellectuals, workers, young people, and diverse social movements unite to create the public spaces and unsettling formative educational cultures necessary for reimagining the meaning of radical democracy. In part, this is a pedagogical project, one that recognizes consciousness, agency, and education as central to any viable notion of politics. It is also a project designed to address, critique, and make visible the commonsense ideologies that enable neoliberal capitalism and other elements of an emergent authoritarianism to function alongside a kind of moral coma and political amnesia at the level of everyday life. But such a project will not take place if the American public cannot recognize how the mechanisms of authoritarianism have had an impact on their lives, restructured negatively the notion of freedom, and corrupted power by placing it largely in the hands of ruling elites, corporations, and different segments of the military and national security state. Such a project must work to develop vigorous social spheres and communities that promote a culture of deliberation, public debate, and critical exchange across a wide variety of cultural and institutional sites in an effort to generate democratic movements for social change. Central to such a project is the attempt to foster a new radical imagination as part of a wider political project to create the conditions for a broad-based social movement that can move beyond the legacy of a fractured left/progressive culture and politics in order to address the totality of the society's problems. This suggests finding a common ground in which challenging diverse forms of oppression, exploitation, and exclusion can become part of a broader challenge to create a radical democracy. We need to develop an educated and informed public—one that embraces a culture of questioning and puts into question society's commanding institutions. Such a citizenry is crucial to the development of a critical formative culture organized around a project of autonomy and mode of politics in which, as Cornelius Castoriadis insists, broader concerns with power and justice are connected to the need "to create citizens who are critical thinkers capable of putting existing institutions into question so that democracy again becomes society's movement…that is to say, a new type of regime in the full sense of the term."[56] We live in a time that demands a discourse of both critique and possibility, one that recognizes that without an informed citizenry, collective struggle, and viable social movements, democracy will slip out of our reach and we will arrive at a new stage of history marked by the birth of an authoritarianism that not only disdains all vestiges of democracy but is more than willing to relegate it to a distant memory.

CONCLUSION

This book was published just as the Obama administration finished its second year in office. Initially, hopes were high among large segments of the American public.

The long dark years of war, repression, secrecy, and corruption were rejected by popular vote, and a brighter day seemed on the horizon, or so it seemed. Obama spoke a political language that embodied hope, and his earnest embrace of the American dream appeared to represent the possibility of a more just future. Under Bush, the United States had come as close to authoritarianism as was possible without giving up all vestiges of democratic aspirations. The Bush/Cheney regime was the apotheosis of a new kind of politics in American life, one in which the arrogance of power and wealth transformed a limited social state into a mode of sovereignty that not only worked in the interests of rich and powerful corporations but also increasingly viewed more and more individuals and groups as disposable and expendable. As politics came to occupy the center of life itself, the welfare state was transformed into a corporate and punishing state. Problems were no longer viewed as in need of social and political remedies. Instead, they were criminalized, reduced to matters of law and order—when law and order weren't suspended altogether. The defense of the common good, public values, and social protections moved from the center of political culture to the margins—reduced to an inconvenience, if not a threat to those who occupied the privileged precincts of power. In the midst of a militarized culture of fear, insecurity, and market-driven values, economics drove politics to its death-dealing limit, as crucial considerations of justice, ethics, and compassion were largely expunged from our political vocabulary, except as objects of disdain or a weak-kneed liberal nostalgic yearning. It seemed as if the living dead now ruled every commanding aspect of the culture, extending from the media to popular expression itself.

Tragically, little has changed since Barack Obama took office. The politics of corruption, death, and despair appear to define the Obama administration as much as they did the relentless eight years of the Bush regime. This book is an attempt to develop a new form of political critique forged out of what may seem an extreme metaphor, the zombie or hyper-dead. Yet the metaphor is particularly apt for drawing attention to the ways in which political culture and power in American society now work in the interests of bare survival, if not disposability, for the vast majority of people—a kind of war machine and biopolitics committed to the creation of death-worlds, a new and unique form of social existence in which large segments of the population live under a state of siege, reduced to a form of social death. The zombie metaphor does more than suggest the symbolic face of power, it points dramatically to a kind of "mad agency that is power in a new form, death-in-life"[57] agency without conscience and bereft of social democratic imagination or hope. This is what Achille Mbembe calls necropolitics in which "death is the mediator of the present—the only form of agency left."[58] What is new about this type of politics is that it is not hidden, lurking in the shadows but appears daily and unremarkably in memos, reports, and policies justifying illegal legalities such as the use of state secrets, indefinite detention without charge, the massive incarceration of people of color, hidden prisons, a world of night raids, the bailout of corrupt corporations that led to the direct destitution of millions, and the full-fledged attack on a weakened oppositional culture of thoughtfulness and critique, itself all but left for dead. The figure of the zombie utilizes the iconography of the living dead to signal a society that appears to have stopped questioning itself, that revels in its collusion with human suffering, and is awash in a culture of unbridled materialism and narcissism. Though not of his making, this is now Obama's challenge; and yet the politics of death and suffering continue unabated both in the United States and in America's imperial adventures abroad.

This book is an attempt to understand critically both the political and peda-gogical conditions that have produced this culture of sadism and death, attempt-ing to mark and chart its visible registers, including the emergence of right-wing teaching machines, a growing politics of disposability, the emergence of a culture of cruelty, the ongoing war being waged on young people, and especially on youth of color. The book begins and ends with an analysis of authoritarianism and the ways it reworks itself, mutates, and attacks parasitically the desiccated shell of democra-cy, sucking out its life-blood. The focus on authoritarianism serves as both a warn-ing as well as a call to critical engagement in the interest of hope—not as a political rhetoric emptied of context and commitment but one that seeks to resuscitate a democratic imaginary and energized social movements that is the one antidote to the zombification of politics.

In the first section of the book, elements of the new authoritarianism are ana-lyzed as a death-dealing politics that works its way through a culture of deceit, fear, humiliation, torture, and market-driven desire for their ever-more "extreme" expres-sions. Next it focuses on challenging the rise of a politics of illiteracy and the ongo-ing destruction of democratic public spheres, stressing how the values of casino capitalism are mobilized through the emergence of market-driven commercial spheres and public institutions such as schools. The third section of the book focus-es on the figure of youth as a register of the crisis of public values, signaling the impending crisis of a democratic future. The merging of zombie politics and the increasing scale of suffering and hardship that young people have to endure in the United States points to the serious political and ethical consequences of a society mobilized and controlled by casino capitalism—a capitalism that in its arrogance and greed takes the side of death and destruction rather than siding with democ-racy and public life. The figure of the zombie signifies not just a crisis of conscious-ness but a new type of political power and "mad agency," visible in the rituals of economic Darwinism that rule not just reality TV but everyday life. But such a pol-itics is far from undefeatable, and surely it is not without the continued presence and possibility of individual and collective resistance. My hope is that this book will break through a diseased common sense that often masks zombie politicians, anti-public intellectuals, politics, institutions, and social relations and bring into focus the need for a new language, pedagogy, and politics in which the living dead will be moved decisively to the margins rather than occupying the very center of politics and everyday life.

NOTES

1. Hannah Arendt, *Between Past and Future* (1968; New York: Penguin Books, 1993), p. 196.
2. I have taken this term from Stephen Jones, ed., *The Dead That Walk* (Berkeley, CA: Ulysses Press, 2010).
3. Editorial, "Wall Street Casino," *The New York Times* (April 28, 2010), p. A24, http://www.nytimes.com/2010/04/28/opinion/28wed1.html.
4. Some of the ideas come from Richard Greene and K. Silem Mohammad, eds., *Zombies, Vampires, and Philosophy: New Life for the Undead* (Chicago: Open Court, 2010).
5. Arun Gupta, "Party of No: How Republicans and the Right Have Tried to Thwart All Social Progress," *Truthout.org* (May 21, 2010), www.alternet.org/news/146965.
6. Jonathan J. Cooper, "We're All Arizonians Now," *Huffington Post* (May 15, 2010), http://www.huffingtonpost.com/2010/05/15/sarah-palin-were-all-ariz_n_577671.html.
7. See the excellent commentary on this issue by Frank Rich, "The Rage Is Not About Health Care," *The New York Times* (March 28, 2010), p. WK10. See also Justine Sharrock, "The Oath Keepers: The Militant and Armed Side of the Tea Party Movement," *AlterNet* (March 6, 2010), http://www.alternet.org/story/145769; and Mark Potok, "Rage on the Right: The Year in Hate and Extremism," *Southern Poverty Law Center Intelligence Report* 137 (Spring 2010), http://www.splcenter.org/get-informed/intelligence-report/browse-all-issues/2010/spring/rage-on-the-right.
8. Paul Krugman, "Going to Extreme," *The New York Times* (May 16, 2010), p. A23.
9. James Traub, "The Way We Live Now: Weimar Whiners," *The New York Times Magazine* (June 1, 2003), http://www.nytimes.com/2003/06/01/magazine/the-way-we-live-now-6-01-03-weimar-whiners.html?scp=2&sq=%E2%80%9CWeimar%20Whiners,%E2%80%9D&st=cse. For a commentary on such intellectuals, see Tony Judt, "Bush's Useful Idiots," *The London Review of Books* 28:18 (September 21, 2006), http://www.lrb.co.uk/v28/n18/tony-judt/bushs-useful-idiots.
10. Cited in Carol Becker, "The Art of Testimony," *Sculpture* (March 1997), p. 28.
11. This case for an American version of authoritarianism was updated and made more visible in a number of interesting books and articles. See, for instance, Chris Hedges, *American Fascists: The Christian Right and the War on America* (New York: Free Press, 2006); Henry A. Giroux, *Against the Terror of Neoliberalism: Politics Beyond the Age of Greed* (Boulder, CO: Paradigm Publishers, 2008); and Sheldon S. Wolin, *Democracy Incorporated: Managed Democracy and the Specter of Inverted Totalitarianism* (Princeton: Princeton University Press, 2008).
12. Cited in Paul Bigioni, "Fascism Then, Fascism Now," *Toronto Star* (November 27, 2005), http://www.informationclearinghouse.info/article11155.htm.
13. See Bertram Gross, *Friendly Fascism: The New Face of Power in America* (Montreal: Black Rose Books, 1985).

14. Robert O. Paxton, *The Anatomy of Fascism* (New York: Alfred A. Knopf, 2004), p. 202.

15. Umberto Eco, "Eternal Fascism: Fourteen Ways of Looking at a Blackshirt," *New York Review of Books* (November–December 1995), p. 15.

16. Wolin, *Democracy Incorporated.*

17. Along similar theoretical lines, see Stephen Lendman, "A Look Back and Ahead: Police State in America," *CounterPunch* (December 17, 2007), http://www.counterpunch.org/ledman12172007.html. For an excellent analysis that points to the creeping power of the national security state on American universities, see David Price, "Silent Coup: How the CIA Is Welcoming Itself Back onto American University Campuses," *CounterPunch* 17:3 (January 13–31, 2010), pp. 1–5.

18. David Harvey, "Organizing for the Anti-Capitalist Transition," *Monthly Review* (December 15, 2009), http://davidharvey.org/2009/12/organizing-for-the-anti-capitalist-transition/.

19. Chris Hedges, "Democracy in America Is a Useful Fiction," *TruthDig* (January 24, 2010), http://www.truthdig.com/report/item/democracy_in_america_is_a_useful_fiction_20100124/?ln

20. See Janine R. Wedel, *Shadow Elite: How the World's New Power Brokers Undermine Democracy, Government, and the Free Market* (New York: Basic Books, 2010).

21. Zygmunt Bauman, *Liquid Times: Living in an Age of Uncertainty* (London: Polity Press, 2007), pp. 57–58.

22. Ibid., p. 64.

23. Bigioni, "Fascism Then, Fascism Now."

24. Cornelius Castoriadis, "The Nature and Value of Equity," *Philosophy, Politics, Autonomy: Essays in Political Philosophy* (New York: Oxford University Press, 1991), pp. 124–142.

25. Thomas L. Friedman, "A Manifesto for the Fast World," *The New York Times Magazine* (March 28, 1999), http://www.nytimes.com/1999/03/28/magazine/a-manifesto-for-the-fast-world.html?scp=1&sq=A%20Manifesto%20for%20the%20Fast%20World&st=cse.

26. Leo Lowenthal, "Atomization of Man," *False Prophets: Studies in Authoritarianism* (New Brunswick, NJ: Transaction Books, 1987), pp. 182–183.

27. Tony Judt, *Ill Fares the Land* (New York: Penguin Press, 2010), pp. 2–3.

28. I have taken up this issue in my *Youth in a Suspect Society: Democracy or Disposability?* (New York: Palgrave, 2009). For a series of brilliant commentaries on youth in America, see the work of Tolu Olorunda in *The Black Commentator, Truthout*, and other online journals.

29. Evelyn Pringle, "Why Are We Drugging Our Kids?," *Truthout* (December 14, 2009), http://www.alternet.org/story/144538.

30. Ibid.

31. See Nicholas Confessore, "New York Finds Extreme Crisis in Youth Prisons," *The New York Times* (December 14, 2009), p. A1; Duff Wilson, "Poor Children Likelier to Get Antipsychotics," *The New York Times* (December 12, 2009), p. A1; and Amy Goodman, "Jailing Kids for Cash," *Truthout* (February 17, 2009), http://www.truthout.org/021909J.

32. Jake Tapper, "Political Punch: Power, Pop, and Probings from ABC News Senior White House Correspondent—Duncan: Katrina Was the 'Best Thing' for New Orleans School System," *ABC News.com* (January 29, 2010), http://blogs.abcnews.com/politicalpunch/2010/01/duncan-katrina-was-the-best-thing-for-new-orleans-schools.html.

33. Nathaniel Cary, "GOP Hopeful: People on Public Assistance 'Like Stray Animals,'" *Truthout* (January 23, 2010), http://www.truthout.org/gop-hopeful-people-public-assistance-like-stray-animals56335.

34. Cited in Frank Rich, "The State of Union Is Comatose," *The New York Times* (January 31, 2010),

p. WK10.

35. See, for example, Patrick J. Buchanan, "Traditional Americans Are Losing Their Nation," *WorldNetDaily* (January 24, 2010), http://www.wnd.com/index.php?pageId=113463.

36. Frank Rich, "The Rage Is Not About Health Care," *The New York Times* (March 28, 2010), p. WK10.

37. Chris Hedges, "Is America 'Yearning for Fascism'?," *TruthDig* (March 29, 2010), http://www.truthdig.com/report/item/is_america_yearning_for_fascism_20100329/.

38. Rich, "The State of the Union Is Comatose," p. WK10.

39. Robert Reich, "Our Incredible Shrinking Democracy," *AlterNet* (February 2, 2010), http://www.alternet.org/story/145512/.

40. Ibid.

41. Wolin, *Democracy Incorporated*, pp. 259–260.

42. Heather Maher, "Majority of Americans Think Torture 'Sometimes' Justified," *Common Dreams* (December 4, 2009), http://www.commondreams.org/headline/2009/12/04–0.

43. See, for example, Kevin Passmore, *Fascism* (London: Oxford University Press, 2002); and Robert O. Paxton, *The Anatomy of Fascism* (New York: Knopf, 2004).

44. Alexander Stille, "The Latest Obscenity Has Seven Letters," *The New York Times* (September 13, 2003), p. 19.

45. Judith Butler, "Uncritical Exuberance?" *IndyBay.org* (November 5, 2008), http://www.indybay.org/newsitems/2008/11/05/18549195.php.

46. For an excellent analysis of the current status of the Patriot Act, see William Fisher, "Patriot Act—Eight Years Later," *Truthout* (February 3, 2010), http://www.truthout.org/patriot-act-eight-years-later56600.

47. Glenn Greenwald has taken up many of these issues in a critical and thoughtful fashion. See his blog at *Salon*: http://www.salon.com/news/opinion/glenn_greenwald/.

48. Noam Chomsky, "Anti-Democratic Nature of US Capitalism Is Being Exposed," *The Irish Times* (October 10, 2008), www.commondreams.org/view/2008/10/10–4.

49. Roger D. Hodge, "The Mendacity of Hope," *Harper's Magazine* (February 2010), pp. 7–8.

50. Chris Hedges, "Democracy in America Is a Useful Fiction," *TruthDig* (January 24, 2010), http://www.truthdig.com/report/item/democracy_in_america_is_a_useful_fiction_20100124/?ln

51. Naomi Klein, "How Corporate Branding Has Taken over America," *The Guardian/UK* (January 16, 2010), http://www.guardian.co.uk/books/2010/jan/16/naomi-klein-branding-obama-america.

52. Wolin, *Democracy Incorporated*, p. 259.

53. Stuart Hall and Les Back, "In Conversation: At Home and Not at Home," *Cultural Studies* 23:4 (July 2009), pp. 664–665.

54. Klein, "How Corporate Branding."

55. Wolin, *Democracy Incorporated*, p. 287.

56. Cornelius Castoriadis, "Democracy as Procedure and Democracy as Regime," *Constellations* 4:1 (1997), p. 4.

57. This quote comes from my colleague David L. Clark in a personal email correspondence.

58. Achille Mbembe, "Necropolitics," *Public Culture* 15:1 (2003), p. 39.

SECTION I

Zombie Politics and the Culture of Cruelty

CHAPTER ONE

Zombie Politics and Other Late Modern Monstrosities in the Age of Disposability

Monsters of disaster are special kinds of divine warning. They are harbingers of things we do not want to face, of catastrophes, and we fear they will bring such events upon us by coming to us.

JANE ANNA GORDON AND LEWIS R. GORDON.[1]

At present Americans are fascinated by a particular kind of monstrosity, by vampires and zombies condemned to live an eternity by feeding off the souls of the living. The preoccupation with such parasitic relations speaks uncannily to the threat most Americans perceive from the shameless blood lust of contemporary captains of industry, which Matt Taibbi, a writer for *Rolling Stone*, has aptly described as "a great vampire squid wrapped around the face of humanity, relentlessly jamming its blood funnel into anything that smells like money."[2] Media culture, as the enormous popularity of the *Twilight* franchise and HBO's *True Blood* reveals, is nonetheless enchanted by this seductive force of such omnipotent beings. More frightening, however, than the danger posed by these creatures is the coming revolution enacted by the hordes of the unthinking, caught in the spell of voodoo economics and compelled to acts of obscene violence and mayhem. They are the living dead, or what I have labeled in the introduction as the hyper-dead, whose contagion threatens the very life force of the nation.

Only a decade or so ago, citizens feared the wrath of robots—terminators and cyborgs who wanted to destroy us—the legacy of a highly rationalized, technocratic culture that eludes human regulation, even comprehension. That moment has passed, and we are now in the 2.0 phase of that same society where instrumental rationality and technocracy threaten the planet as never before. But now, those who are not part of a technocratic elite appear helpless and adrift, trapped in the grip of a society that denies them any alternative sense of politics or hope. Caught in a society increasingly marked by massive inequality and the divide between the privileged spaces of gated communities and the dead space of "broken highways, bankrupt cities, collapsing bridges, failed schools, the unemployed, the underpaid and the uninsured,"[3] the armies of disposable populations are condemned to roam the shattered American landscape with a blind and often unthinking rage.

Zombies are invading almost every aspect of our daily lives. Not only are the flesh-chomping, blood-lusting, pale-faced creatures with mouths full of black goo appearing in movie theaters, television series, and everywhere in screen culture as shock advertisements, but these flesh-eating zombies have become an apt metaphor for the current state of American politics. Not only do zombies portend a new aesthetic in which hyper-violence is embodied in the form of a carnival of snarling creatures engoring elements of human anatomy, but they also portend the arrival of a revolting politics that has a ravenous appetite for spreading destruction and promoting human suffering and hardship.[4] This is a politics in which cadres of the unthinking and living dead promote civic catastrophes and harbor apocalyptic visions, focusing more on death than life. Death-dealing zombie politicians and their acolytes support modes of corporate and militarized governance through which entire populations now become redundant, disposable, or criminalized. This is especially true for poor minority youth, who as flawed consumers and unwanted workers, are offered the narrow choice of joining the military, going to prison, or are simply being exiled into various dead zones in which they become socially embedded and invisible.[5] Zombie values find expression in an aesthetic that is aired daily in the mainstream media, a visual landscape filled with the spectacle of destruction and decay wrought by human parasites in the form of abandoned houses, cars, gutted cities and trashed businesses. There are no zombie-free spaces in this version of politics. Paralyzed by fear, American society has become the site of a series of planned precision attacks on constitutional rights, dissent, and justice itself. Torture, kidnappings, secret prisons, preventive detention, illegal domestic spying, and the dissolution of habeas corpus have become the protocol of a newly fashioned dystopian mode of governance. Zombie politics reveals much about the gory social and political undercurrent of American society.

This is a politics in which the undead—or, more aptly, the living dead—rule and rail against any institution, set of values, and social relations that embrace the common good or exhibit compassion for the suffering of others. Zombie politics supports megacorporations that cannibalize the economy, feeding off taxpayer dollars while undercutting much-needed spending for social services. The vampires of Wall Street reach above and beyond the trajectories of traditional politics, exercising an influence that has no national or civic allegiance, displaying an arrogance that is as unchecked as its power is unregulated. As Maureen Dowd has pointed out, one particularly glaring example of such arrogance can be found in Lloyd Blankfein's response to a reporter's question when he asked the chief of Goldman Sachs if "it is possible to make too much money."[6] Blankfein responded by insisting, without irony, that he—and I presume his fellow Wall Street vampires—were "doing God's work,"[7] a response truly worthy of one of the high priests of voodoo economics who feels no remorse and offers no apology for promoting a global financial crisis while justifying a bloated and money-obsessed culture of greed and exploitation that has caused enormous pain, suffering, and hardship for millions of people. Unfortunately, victim to their own voodoo economics, the undead—along with their financial institutions, which were once barely breathing, keep coming back, even when it appears that the zombie banks and investment houses have failed one last time, with no hope of once again wreaking their destruction upon society.

Zombie ideologies proliferate like the breathing, blood-lusting corpses in the classic *Night of the Living Dead*. They spew out toxic gore that supports the market as the organizing template for all institutional and social relations, mindlessly compelled, it seems, to privatize everything and aim invective at the idea of big government but never at the notion of the bloated corporate and militarized state. Zombie culture hates big government, a euphemism for the social state, but loves big corporations and is infatuated with the ideology that, in zombieland, unregulated banks, insurance companies, and other megacorporations should make major decisions not only about governing society but also about who is privileged and who is disposable, who should live and who should die. Zombie politics rejects the welfare state for a hybridized corporate and punishing state. Just as it views any vestige of a social safety net as a sign of weakness, if not pathology, its central message seems to be that we are all responsible for ourselves and that the war of all against all is at the core of the apocalyptic vision that makes zombie politics both appealing as a spectacle and convincing as a politics. Zombie violence and policies are everywhere, backed by an army of zombie economic advisors, lobbyists, and legislators, all of whom seem to revel in spreading the culture of the undead while feasting on the spread of war, human suffering, violence, and catastrophe across the United States and the larger globe.

Evidence of the long legacy of zombie politics and its death-dealing policies is on full display as we move into the mid-stages of the Obama administration. Even progressive zombie books such as Max Brooks's *World War Z* have a hard time keeping up with the wrath of destruction overtaking American society, especially as the mutually determining forces of economic inequality, corporate power, and a growing punishing corporate state become the defining features of zombie politics at the beginning of the new millennium. It is a millennium, in this case, marked by a burgeoning landscape filled with the wreckage of those populations now considered excess, especially with regard to children, who are increasingly treated as one of the most disposable populations. For instance, the Obama administration now labors under the burden of death-dealing institutions and advisors, along with a predatory market-driven economics that continues to produce an economic recession in which over 13 million children live in poverty, 17 percent of poor children lack insurance, nearly half of all children and 90 percent of black youth will be on food stamps at some point in their youth, 45,000 people die every year because of a lack of health insurance, 3.6 million elderly live in poverty, and more than 16 million people are unemployed. The violence of zombie politics is also evident in the fact that more and more working- and middle-class youth and poor youth of color find themselves confronted with either vastly diminishing opportunities or are fed into an ever-expanding system of disciplinary control that dehumanizes, medicalizes, and criminalizes their behavior in multiple sites, extending from the home and school to the criminal justice system—not, of course, devoured in order to be "integrated" or "incorporated" into the system but rather ingested and vomited up, thus securing the permanence of their exclusion.

With the cruelest of ironies, zombie politics and culture invoke life as they promote death and human suffering. For example, zombie politicians who oppose the welfare state, health care reform, investing in a quality education for all children, rebuilding the nation's crumbling infrastructure, and creating a federally funded jobs program for young people and the unemployed often argue that they oppose such programs because they will saddle the next generation with a massive debt. And yet, they have no regrets about funding wars in Afghanistan and Iraq that since 2001 have cost American taxpayers over $930 billion dollars. Nor is there any remorse for supporting under the Clinton and Bush administrations massive tax breaks for the rich that reduced government revenue by trillions of dollars. In their embrace of market deregulation, do they say or do anything about a food industry "that is spending millions of dollars on slick digital marketing campaigns promoting fatty and sugary products to teenagers and children on the Internet, on cell phones and even inside video games—often without the knowledge of parents"?[8] Nor do the zombie politicians utter a whisper about a country that is singularly responsible for jailing over 2,500 juvenile offenders for life without the possibility of parole or address the shameful fact that "just over 100 people in the world [are] serving sentences of life without the possibility of parole for crimes they committed as juveniles in which no one was killed [and that all] are in the United States."[9] Instead, zombie politicians, blood-sucking C.E.O.s, and media pundits resort to deceit and misrepresentation while reproducing a culture of deception and cruelty. This is the group that—even as they invoked death panels and denied their own morbid predilections—warned before the passing of the health care reform bill that such legislation was largely "stealthy reparations for slavery." And one true representative of the hyper-dead, Rep. Virginia Foxx, R-N.C, proclaimed without the slightest hint of self-reflection that "there are no Americans who don't have health care."[10] Foxx rates high as one of the zombie politicians spewing forth the kind of blood-soaked venom that would make even the most hardened hyper-dead cringe. She has not only argued that health care reform poses a greater threat to the United States than "any terrorist right now in any country." She has also, as Joshua Holland points out, insisted that health care reform "would be just like an ax-murderer crawling into the room of a small, defenseless child in the dark of night, only much scarier."[11]

One of the cardinal policies of zombie politics is to redistribute wealth upward to produce record-high levels of inequality, just as corporate power is simultaneously consolidated at a speed that threatens to erase the most critical gains made over the last fifty years to curb the anti-democratic power of corporations. And yet this uncritical celebration of market fundamentalism, with its profound disdain for the common good, seems to revel in the human suffering caused by conditions of endemic inequality, which as Tony Judt rightly argues "is the pathology of the age and the greatest threat to the health of any democracy." [12] Zombie policies aimed at hollowing out the social state are now matched by an increase in repressive legislation to curb the unrest that might explode among those populations falling into the despair and suffering unleashed by a "savage, fanatical capitalism" that constitutes a war against the public good, the welfare state, and "social citizenship."[13]

Deregulation, privatization, commodification, corporate mergers, and asset stripping go hand in hand with the curbing of civil liberties, the increasing criminalization of social problems, and the fashioning of the prison as the preeminent space of racial containment. (One in nine black males between the ages of 20 and 34 is incarcerated.[14]) The alleged morality of market freedom is now secured through the ongoing immorality of a militarized state that embraces torture, war, and violence as legitimate functions of political sovereignty and the ordering of daily life. As corporations increase their profits and power, the rich get richer, and the reach of the punishing state extends itself further, those forces and public spheres that once provided a modicum of protection for workers, the poor, sick, aged, and young are undermined, leaving large numbers of people impoverished and with little hope for the future.

David Harvey refers to this primary feature of zombie politics as "accumulation by dispossession,"[15] which encompasses the privatization and commodification of public assets, deregulation of the financial sector, and the use of the state to direct the flow of wealth upward through, among other practices, tax policies that favor the rich and cut back the social wage. As Harvey points out, "All of these processes amount to the transfer of assets from the public and popular realms to the private and class privileged domains"[16] and to the overwhelming of political institutions by powerful corporations that keep them in check. Zygmunt Bauman goes further and argues that not only do zombie politics and predatory capitalism draw their life blood from the relentless process of asset stripping, but they also produce "the acute crisis of the 'human waste' disposal industry, as each new outpost conquered by capitalist markets adds new thousands or millions to the mass of men and women already deprived of their lands, workshops, and communal safety nets."[17] The upshot of such policies is that larger segments of the population are now struggling under the burden of massive debt, bankruptcy, unemployment, lack of adequate health care, and a brooding sense of hopelessness. Once again, what is unique about this type of zombie politics is not merely the anti-democratic notion that the market should be the guide for all human actions but also the sheer hatred for any form of sovereignty in which the government could promote the general welfare. Zombie politics and the devaluation of the public good go hand in hand.

As Thom Hartmann points out, zombie politics has given way to punishment as one of the central features of governing. He describes the policies that flow from such politics as follows: "Government should punish, they agree, but it should never nurture, protect, or defend individuals. Nurturing and protecting, they suggest, is the more appropriate role of religious institutions, private charities, families, and—perhaps most important—corporations. Let the corporations handle your old-age pension. Let the corporations decide how much protection we and our environment need from their toxins. Let the corporations decide what we're paid. Let the corporations decide what doctor we can see, when, and for what purpose."[18] But zombie politics and the punishing state do more than substitute charity and private aid for government-backed social provisions while they criminalize a range of existing social problems. They also cultivate a culture of fear and suspicion toward all those others—immigrants, refugees, Muslims, youth, minorities of class and color, the unemployed, the disabled, and the elderly—who, in the absence of dense social networks and social supports, fall prey to unprecedented levels of displaced resentment from the media, public scorn for their vulnerability, and increased criminalization because social protections are considered too costly, thus rendering these groups both dangerous and unfit for integration into American society. Loïc Wacquant argues that the rise of the punishing state correlates with the crisis of the welfare state and that welfare agencies and penal policies now work together in offering "relief not *to* the poor *but from* the poor, by forcibly "disappearing" the most disruptive of them, from the shrinking welfare rolls on the one hand and into the swelling dungeons of the carceral castle on the other."[19] Prisons in this view have now become a primary constituent of the neoliberal state. Coupled with this rewriting of the obligations of sovereign-state power and the transfer of sovereignty to the market is a widely endorsed assumption that regardless of the suffering, misery, and problems visited on human beings by these arrangements, they are not only responsible for their fate but reliant ultimately on themselves for survival. There is more at stake here than the vengeful return of an older colonial fantasy that regarded the natives as less than human or the now-ubiquitous figure of the disposable worker as a prototypical by-product of the casino capitalist order—though the histories of racist and class-based exclusion inform the withdrawal of moral and ethical concerns from these populations.[20] What we are currently witnessing in this form of zombie politics and predatory capitalism is the unleashing of a powerfully regressive symbolic and corporeal violence against all those individuals and groups who have been "othered" because their very presence undermines the engines of wealth and inequality that drive the neoliberal dreams of consumption, power, and profitability for the very few. While the state still has the power of the law to reduce individuals to impoverishment and to strip them of civil rights, due process, and civil liberties, zombie politics increasingly wields its own form of sovereignty through the invisible hand of the market, which has the power to produce new configurations of control, regulate social health, and alter human life in unforeseen and profound ways. Zygmunt Bauman's analysis of how market sovereignty differs from traditional modes of state sovereignty is worth citing in full.

> This strange sovereign [the market] has neither legislative nor executive agencies, not to mention courts of law—which are rightly viewed as the indispensable paraphernalia of the bona fide sovereigns explored and described in political science textbooks. In consequence, the market is, so to speak, more sovereign than the much advertised and eagerly self-advertising political sovereigns, since in addition to returning the verdicts of exclusion, the market allows for no appeals procedure. Its sentences are as firm and irrevocable as they are informal, tacit, and seldom if ever spelled out in writing. Exemption by the organs of a sovereign state can be objected to and protested against, and so stands a chance of being annulled—but not eviction by the sovereign market, because no presiding judge is named here, no receptionist is in sight to accept appeal papers, while no address has been given to which they could be mailed.[21]

Traditional modes of liberal politics recognized democracy's dependency on the people it governed and to whom it remained accountable. But no one today votes for which corporations have the right to dominate the media and filter the information made available to the public; there is no electoral process that determines how private companies grant or deny people access to adequate health care and other social services. The reign of the market shapes conditions of life and death in a zombie economy. It is not restricted to a limited term of appointment, despite the market's unprecedented sovereignty over the lives of citizens in democratic countries—sovereignty essentially defined as the "power and capacity to dictate who may live and who may die."[22] This shift to market sovereignty, values, and power points to the importance of zombie politics as an attempt to think through not only how politics uses power to mediate the convergence of life and death, but also how sovereign power proliferates those conditions in which individuals marginalized by race, class, and gender configurations are "stripped of political significance and exposed to murderous violence."[23]

Under such circumstances, it is more crucial than ever to develop a politics of resistance that echoes Theodor Adorno's argument that "the undiminished presence of suffering, fear, and menace necessitates that the thought that cannot be realized should not be discarded ... [that individuals and citizens] must come to know, without any mitigation, why the world—which could be paradise here and now—can become hell itself tomorrow."[24] If Adorno is right, and I think he is, the task ahead is to fashion a more critical and redemptive notion of politics, one that takes seriously the emergence of a form of social death that is becoming the norm rather than the exception for many Americans and at the same time refuses to accept, even in its damaged forms, an apocalyptic zombie politics and its accompanying culture of fear, its endless spectacles of violence that promote airtight forms of domination. We need new political and educational narratives about what is possible in terms of producing a different future, especially for young people, what it means to promote new modes of social responsibility, and what it takes to create sites and strategies in which resistance to zombie politics becomes possible. Starting with how we might fight for real economic, institutional, and structural reforms in the interest of children is not without merit for envisioning the broader reforms necessary in an aspiring democracy.

At the very least, this suggests fighting for a child welfare system that would reduce "family poverty by increasing the minimum wage," institute "a guaranteed income, provide high-quality subsidized child care, preschool education, and paid parental leaves for all families."[25] Young people need a federally funded jobs creation program and wage subsidy that would provide year-round employment for out-of-school youth and summer jobs that target in-school, low-income youth. Public and higher education, increasingly defined by corporate and military agendas, must be reclaimed as democratic public spheres that educate young people about how to govern rather than merely be governed. Incarceration should be the last resort, not the first recourse for dealing with our children. We need to get the police out of public schools, greatly reduce spending for prisons, and hire more teachers, support staff, and community people in order to eliminate the school-to-prison pipeline. In order to make life livable for young people and others, basic supports must be put in place, such as a system of national health insurance that covers everybody, along with affordable housing. At the very least, we need guaranteed health care for young people, and we need to lower the age of eligibility for Medicare to

55 in order to keep poor families from going bankrupt. And, of course, none of this will take place unless the institutions, power relations, and values that legitimate and reproduce current levels of inequality, power, and human suffering are dismantled. The widening gap between the rich and the poor has to be addressed if young people are to have a viable future. Ensuring this future for our children will require pervasive structural reforms that constitute a real shift in both power and politics away from a market-driven system that views too many young people and other vulnerable populations as disposable. Against a zombie politics and a predatory capitalism, we need to reimagine what liberty, equality, and freedom might mean as truly democratic values and practices.

Notes

1. Jane Anna Gordon and Lewis R. Gordon, *Of Divine Warning: Reading Disaster in the Modern Age* (Boulder, CO: Paradigm Publishers, 2009), p. 10.
2. Matt Taibbi, "The Great American Bubble Machine," *Rolling Stone* (July 13, 2009), http://www.rollingstone.com/politics/story/29127316/the_great_american_bubble_machine.
3. Tony Judt, *Ill Fares the Land* (New York: Penguin Press, 2010), p. 12.
4. The relationship between zombies and the politics of culture has been explored in David Sirota, "Zombie Zeitgeist: Why Undead Corpses Are Dominating at the Box Office," *AlterNet* (October 8, 2009), http://www.alternet.org/media/143179/zombie_zeitgeist:_why_undead_corpses_are_dominating _at_the_box_office/. See also, Stephen Jones, ed., *The Dead That Walk* (Berkeley, CA: Ulysses Press, 2010).
5. On this issue, see Christopher Robbins, *Expelling Hope: The Assault on Youth and the Militarization of Schooling* (Albany: SUNY Press, 2008) and Ken Saltman, *The Edison School: Corporate Schooling and the Assault on Public Education* (New York: Routledge, 2005). Also see my *Youth in a Suspect Society: Democracy or Disposability?* (New York: Palgrave Macmillan, 2009).
6. Cited in Maureen Dowd, "Virtuous Bankers? Really!?!," *The New York Times* (November 11, 2009), p. A27.
7. Ibid.
8. Dan Harris, Suzanne Yeo, Christine Brouwer, and Joel Siegel, "Marketing Has Eye on Kids' Tastes for Food, 'Net,'" *ABC News* (November 1, 2009), http://abcnews.go.com/WN/w_ParentingResource/vigilant-parents-unaware-marketingtechniques-draw-teens-kids/story?id=8969255.
9. Adam Liptak, "Justices Weigh Life in Prison for Youths Who Never Killed," *The New York Times* (November 8, 2009), p. A1. For an excellent analysis of this issue that focuses on one particularly tragic case, see Tolu Olorunda, "Sarah Kruzan: 16-Year-Old Sentenced to Life for Killing Pimp," *The Daily Voice* (October 26, 2009), http://thedailyvoice.com/voice/2009/10/sarah-kruzan-16yearold-sentenc-002362.php.
10. Joshua Holland, "10 of the Nuttiest Statements Elected Officials Have Made in the Health Care Battle," *AlterNet* (November 7, 2009), http://www.alternet.org/politics/143790/10_of_the_nuttiest_statements_elected_officials_have_ made_in_the_health_care_battle/.
11. Ibid.
12. Tony Judt, *Ill Fares the Land* (New York: Penguin Press, 2010), p. 160.

13. Mike Davis and Daniel Bertrand Monk, eds., "Introduction," *Evil Paradises* (New York: The New Press, 2007), p. ix.
14. See Associated Press, "A First: 1 in 100 Americans Jailed," *MSNBC.com* (February 28, 2008), http://www.msnbc.msn.com/id/23392251/print/1/displaymode/1098/.
15. David Harvey, *A Brief History of Neoliberalism* (New York: Oxford University Press, 2005), p. 7.
16. Ibid., p. 161.
17. Zygmunt Bauman, *Liquid Times: Living in an Age of Uncertainty* (London: Polity Press, 2007), p. 28.
18. Thom Hartmann, "You Can't Govern if You Don't Believe in Government," *CommonDreams.Org* (September 6, 2005), http://www.commondreams.org/views05/0906-21.htm.
19. Loic Wacquant, *Punishing the Poor: The Neoliberal Government of Social Insecurity*, (Durham, NC: Duke University Press, 2009), pp. 294–295
20. Some of the best work on racist exclusion can be found in David Theo Goldberg, *Racist Culture* (Malden, MA: Blackwell, 1993); and David Theo Goldberg, *The Threat of Race: Reflections on Racial Neoliberalism* (Malden, MA: Blackwell, 2009).
21. Zygmunt Bauman, *Consuming Life* (London: Polity Press, 2007), p. 65.
22. Achille Mbembe, "Necropolitics," trans. Libby Meintjes, *Public Culture* 15:1 (2003), pp. 11–12.
23. Ewa Plonowska Ziarek, "Bare Life on Strike: Notes on the Biopolitics of Race and Gender," *South Atlantic Quarterly* 107:1 (Winter 2008), p. 90.
24. Theodor W. Adorno, *Critical Models: Interventions and Catchwords*, trans. Henry W. Pickford (New York: Columbia University Press, 1998), p. 14.
25. Dorothy Roberts, *Shattered Bonds: The Color of Child Welfare* (New York: Basic Books, 2008), p. 268.

CHAPTER TWO

The Politics of Lying and the Culture of Deceit in Obama's America

The Rule of Damaged Politics

Lies are often much more plausible, more appealing to reason, than reality, since the liar has the great advantage of knowing beforehand what the audience wishes or expects to hear.

HANNAH ARENDT[1]

In the current American political landscape, truth is not merely misrepresented or falsified, it is overtly mocked. As is well known, the Bush administration repeatedly lied to the American public, furthering a legacy of government mistrust while carrying the practice of distortion to new and almost unimaginable heights. Even now, within a few years of Bush's leaving office, it is difficult to forget the lies and government-sponsored deceits in which it was claimed that Saddam Hussein had weapons of mass destruction, Iraq was making deals with Al-Qaeda, and, perhaps the most infamous of all, the United States did not engage in torture. Unlike many former administrations, the Bush administration was engaged in pure political theater,[2] giving new meaning to Hannah Arendt's claim that "Truthfulness has never been counted among the political virtues, and lies have always been regarded as justifiable tools in political dealings."[3] For instance, when the government wasn't lying to promote dangerous policies, it willfully produced and circulated fake news reports in order to provide the illusion that the lies and the policies that flowed from them were supported by selective members of the media and the larger public. The Bush deceits and lies were almost never challenged by right-wing media "patriots," who were too busy denouncing as un-American anyone who questioned

Bush's official stream of deception and deceit. Ironically, some of these pundits were actually on the government payroll for spreading the intellectual equivalent of junk food.

In such circumstances, language loses any viable sense of referentiality, while lying, misrepresentation, and the deliberate denial of truth become acceptable practices firmly entrenched in the Wild West of talk radio, cable television, and the dominant media. Fact-finding, arguments bolstered by evidence, and informed analysis have always been fragile entities, but they risk annihilation in a culture in which it becomes difficult to distinguish between an opinion and an argument. Knowledge is increasingly controlled by a handful of corporations and public relations firms and is systemically cleansed of any complexity. Lying and deceitfulness are all too often viewed as just another acceptable tactic in what has become most visibly the pathology of politics and a theater of cruelty dominated by a growing chorus of media hate-mongers inflaming an authoritarian populist rage laced with a not-too-subtle bigotry.[4]

Truth increasingly becomes the enemy of democracy because it does not support the spectacle and the reduction of citizens either to mere dupes of power or commodities. Ignorance is no longer a liability in a culture in which lying, deceit, and misinformation blur the boundaries between informed judgments and the histrionics of a shouting individual or mob. Talk radio and television talk show screamers such as Rush Limbaugh, Michael Savage, and Glenn Beck, in particular, seem to delight in repeating claims that have been discredited in the public arena, demonstrating a barely disguised contempt for both the truth and any viable vestige of journalism. These lies and deceits go beyond the classic political gambit, beyond the Watergate-style cover up, beyond the comic "I did not have sex with that woman." The lies and deceptions that are spewed out every day from the right-wing teaching machines—from newspapers and radio shows to broadcast media and the Internet—capitalize on both the mobilizing power of the spectacle, the increasing impatience with reason, and an obsession with what Susan J. Douglas describes as the use of "provocative sound bites over investigative reporting, misinformation over fact."[5] Lying and deception have become so commonplace in the dominant press that such practices appear to have no moral significance and provoke few misgivings, even when they have important political consequences.

In the age of public relations managers and talk show experts, we are witnessing the demise of public life. At a time when education is reduced to training workers and is stripped of any civic ideals and critical practices, it becomes unfashionable for the public to think critically. Rather than intelligence uniting us, a collective ignorance of politics, culture, the arts, history, and important social issues, as Mark Slouka points out, "gives us a sense of community, it confers citizenship."[6] Our political passivity is underscored by a paucity of intellectual engagement, just as the need for discrete judgment and informed analysis falls prey to a culture of watching, a culture of illusion and circus tricks. Shame over the lying and ignorance that now shape our cultural politics has become a source of national pride—witness the pathetic response to Joe Wilson's outburst against President Obama. Or, for that matter, the celebrated and populist response to Sarah Palin's lies about death panels, which are seized upon not because they distort the truth and reveal the dishonesty and vileness of political opportunism—while also unsuccessfully attempting to undermine a viable health care bill—but because they tap into a sea of growing anger and hyped-up ignorance and ratchet up poll ratings. Lying and deceit have become the stuff of spectacle and are on full display in a society where gossip and celebrity culture rule. In this instance, the consequences of lying are reduced to a matter of prurience rather than public concern, becoming a source of private injury on the part of a Hollywood star or producing the individual humiliation of a public figure such as John Edwards.

The widespread acceptance of lying and deceit is not merely suggestive of a commodified and ubiquitous corporate-driven electronic culture that displays an utter contempt for morality and social needs: it also registers the existence of a troubling form of infantilization and depoliticization. Lying as common sense and deceit as politics-as-usual join the embrace of provocation in a coupling that empties politics and agency of any substance and feeds into a corporate state and militarized culture in which matters of judgment, thoughtfulness, morality, and compassion seem to disappear from public view. What is the social cost of such flight from reality, if not the death of democratic politics, critical thought, and civic agency? When a society loses sight of the distinction between fact and fiction, truth-telling and lying, what happens is that truth, critical thought, and fact-finding as conditions of democracy are rendered trivial and reduced to a collection of mere platitudes, which in turn reinforces moral indifference and political impotence. Under such circumstances, language actually becomes the mechanism for promoting political powerlessness. Lying and deceit are no longer limited to merely substituting falsehoods for the truth; they now performatively constitute their own truth, promoting celebrity culture, right-wing paranoia, and modes of government and corporate power freed from any sense of accountability.

While all governments resort to misrepresentations and lies, we appear to have entered a brave new world in which lies, distortions, and exaggerations have become so commonplace that when something is said by a politician, it is often meant to suggest its opposite, and without either irony or apology. As lies and deceit become a matter of policy, language loses its grip on reality, and the resulting indeterminacy of meaning is often used by politicians and others to embrace positions that change from one moment to the next. Witness Dick Cheney, who once referred to torture as "enhanced interrogation" so as to sugarcoat its brutality and then appeared on national television in 2009 only to defend torture by arguing that if such practices work, they are perfectly justified, even if they violate the law. This is the same Cheney who, appearing on the May 31, 2005, *Larry King Live* show, attempted to repudiate charges of government torture by claiming, without irony, that the detainees "have been well treated, treated humanely and decently." This type of discourse recalls George Orwell's dystopian world of *1984* in which the Ministry of Truth produces lies and the Ministry of Love tortures people. Remember when the Bush administration used the "Healthy Forest Initiative" to give loggers access to protected wilderness areas or the "Clear Skies Initiative" to enable greater industrial air pollution? Former New York City Mayor Rudy Giuliani, appearing on ABC's *Good Morning America* in January 2010, embraced one of the most sordid lies of the year with his claim that "We had no domestic attacks under Bush," as if the attacks on 9/11 never happened. Of course, there is a certain irony here given that he never stopped referring to 9/11 as a way to shamelessly mobilize support for his own failed presidential bid. President Obama also indulges in this kind of semantic dishonesty when he substitutes "prolonged detention" for the much-maligned "preventive detention" policies he inherited from the Bush-Cheney regime. While Obama is not Bush, the use of this type of duplicitous language calls to mind the Orwellian nightmare in which "war is peace, freedom is slavery, and ignorance is strength."

When lying and deceit become normalized in a culture, they serve as an index of how low we have fallen as a literate and civilized society. Such practices also demonstrate the degree to which language and education have become corrupted, tied to corporate and political power, and sabotaged by rigid ideologies as part of a growing authoritarianism that uses the educational force of the culture, the means of communication, and the sites in which information circulate to mobilize ignorance among a misinformed citizenry, all the while supporting reactionary policies. Especially since the horrible events of September 11, 2001, Americans have been encouraged to identify with a militaristic way of life, to suspend their ability to read the word and world critically, to treat corporate and government power in almost religious terms, and to view a culture of questioning as something alien and poisonous to American society. Shared fears rather than shared responsibilities now mobilize angry mobs and gun-toting imbeciles who are praised as "real" Americans. Fear bolstered by lies and manufactured deceptions makes us immune to even the most obvious moral indecencies, such as the use of taser guns on kids in schools. Nobody notices or cares, and one cause and casualty of all of this moral indifference is that language has been emptied of its critical content just as the public spaces that make it possible are disappearing into the arms of corporations, advertisers, and other powerful institutions that show nothing but contempt for either the public sphere or the kind of critical literacy that gives it meaning.

Obama's presence on the national political scene gave literacy, language, and critical thought a newfound sense of dignity, interlaced as they were with a vision of hope, justice, and possibility—and reasonable arguments about the varied crises America faced. But as Obama compromised, if not surrendered, some of his principles to those individuals and groups that live in the language of duplicity, the idealism that shaped his vocabulary began to look like just another falsehood when measured against his continuation of a number of Bush-like policies. In this case, the politics of distortion and misrepresentation that Obama's lack of integrity has produced may prove to be even more dangerous than what we got under Bush, because it wraps itself in a moralism that seems uplifting and hopeful while supporting policies that reward the rich, reduce schools to testing centers, and continue to waste lives and money on wars that should have ended when Obama assumed his presidency. Obama claims he is for peace, and yet the United States is the largest arms dealer in the world. He claims he wants to reduce the deficit but instead spends billions on the defense industry and wars abroad. He says he wants everyone to have access to decent health care but makes backroom deals with powerful pharmaceutical companies. Orwell's ghost haunts this new president and the country at large. Reducing the critical power of language has been crucial to this effort. Under such circumstances, democracy as either a moral referent or a political ideal appears to have lost any measure of credibility. The politics of lying and the culture of deceit are inextricably related to a theater of cruelty and modes of corrupt power in which politics is reduced to a ritualized incantation, just as matters of governance are removed from real struggles over meaning and power.

Beyond disinformation and disguise, the politics of lying and the culture of deceit trade in and abet the rhetoric of fear in order to manipulate the public into a state of servile political dependency and unquestioning ideological support. Fear (and its attendant use of moral panics) not only creates a rhetorical umbrella to promote right-wing ideological agendas (increased military spending, tax relief for the rich, privatization, market-driven reforms, and religious intolerance) but also contributes to a sense of helplessness and cynicism throughout the body politic. The collapse of any vestige of critical literacy, reason, and sustained debate gives way to falsehoods and forms of ignorance that find expression in the often-racist discourse of what Bob Herbert calls "the moronic maestros of right wing radio and TV"[7] endlessly haranguing the public to resist any trace of reason. How else to explain the actions of parents who refuse to let their children listen to a speech on education by, should I say it, an African American president? How else to fathom the dominant media repeating uncritically the views of right-wing groups that portray Obama as Hitler or Stalin or consistently making references that compare him to a gorilla or indulge in other crude racist references? In recent days, these groups have been given ample media attention, as if their opinions are not simply ventriloquizing the worst species of ignorance and racism.

The politics of lying and the culture of deceit are wrapped in the logic of absolute certainty, an ominous harbinger of a kind of illiteracy in which one no longer has to be accountable for justifying opinions, claims, or alleged arguments. Stripped of accountability, language finds its final resting place in a culture of deceit and arrogance in which lying either is accepted as a political strategy or is viewed as simply another normalized aspect of everyday life. The lack of criticism surrounding both government practices and corporations that now exercise unparalleled forms of power is more than shameful; it is an utter capitulation to an Orwellian rhetoric that only thinly veils an egregious form of authoritarianism and racism. In the face of such events, we must develop a critical discourse to address the gap between rhetoric and deeds of those who hold economic, political, and social power. As Hannah Arendt has argued, debate is central to a democratic politics, along with the public space in which individuals can argue, exercise critical judgment, and clarify their relationship to democratic values and public commitments. Critical consciousness and autonomy are, after all, not merely the stuff of political awareness but what makes democratic accountability possible in the first place. They are also the foundation and precondition for individuals, parents, community groups, and social movements to mobilize against such political and moral corruptions.

Democracy is fragile and its fate is always uncertain, but during the last decade we have witnessed those in commanding political and corporate positions exhibit an utter disregard for the truth, morality, and critical debate. The Enron template of lying and deception has turned an ethos of dialogue and persuasion into its opposite: dogmatism and propaganda. In doing so, the American public has been bombarded by a discourse of fear, hate, and racism, coupled with a politics of lying that undermines any viable vestige of a democratic ethos. We now find ourselves living in a society in which right-wing extremists not only wage a war against the truth but also seek to render human beings less than fully human by taking away their desire for justice, spiritual meaning, freedom, and individuality.

Politics must become more attentive to those everyday conditions that have allowed the American public to remain complicitous with such barbaric policies and practices. Exposing the underlying conditions and symptoms of a culture of lying and deceit is both a political and a pedagogical task that demands that people speak out and break through the haze of official discourse, media-induced amnesia, and the fear-producing lies of corrupt politicians and the swelling ranks of hatemongers. The politics of lying and deceit at the current historical moment offers up the specter of not just government abuse, mob hysteria, and potential violence, but also an incipient authoritarianism, one that avidly seeks to eliminate intelligent deliberation, informed public discussion, engaged criticism, and the very possibility of freedom and a vital democratic politics. The spirit of critique is meaningless without literacy and an informed public. For such a public to flourish, it must be supported with public debate and informed agents capable of becoming both witnesses to injustice and forces for transforming those political, economic, and institutional conditions that impose silence and perpetuate human suffering. The distortions, misrepresentations, and lies that have become an integral part of American culture present a serious threat to an aspiring democracy, because they further what John Dewey called the "eclipse of the public," just as they empty politics of its democratic values, meanings, and possibilities.

The hate, extremism, and pathology that have come to define our national political and popular landscapes—heard repeatedly in the prattle of Sarah Palin and Glenn Beck, to name only two of the most popular examples—are legitimated by an appeal to absolute certainty, which becomes the backdrop against which a politics of lying and a culture of deceit, fear, cruelty, and repression flourish. We are witnessing in the politics of lying and the culture of deceit a disconnection between language and social responsibility, politics and critical education, market interests and democratic values, privately felt pain and joys and larger public considerations. Under such circumstances morality becomes painless, if not invisible, while social responsibility is erased from the vocabulary of mainstream politics and the dominant cultural apparatus. And this undermining of the value of human dignity, truth, dialogue, and critical thought is the offspring of a debate over much more than simply meaning and language, or even the widespread legitimacy of individual and institutional ignorance and corruption. At its core it is a debate about power and those corporate and political interests that create the conditions in which lying becomes acceptable and deceit commonplace—those forces that have the power to frame in increasingly narrow ways the conventions, norms, language, and relations through which we relate to ourselves and others.

How we define ourselves as a nation cannot be separated from the language we value, inhabit, and use to shape our understanding of others and the world in which we want to live. As the language of critique, civic responsibility, political courage, and democracy disappears along with sustained investments in schools, media, and other elements of a formative culture that keeps an aspiring democracy alive, we lose the spaces and capacities to imagine a future in which language, literacy, and hope are on the side of justice, rather than on the side of hate, willful ignorance, and widespread injustice.

NOTES

1. Hannah Arendt, "Lying in Politics," in *Crisis of the Republic* (New York: Harvest/HBJ Books, 1969), p. 6.
2. Frank Rich, *The Greatest Story Ever Sold* (New York: Penguin, 2007).

3. Arendt, "Lying in Politics," p. 4.
4. See Bob Herbert's courageous article, "The Scourge Persists," *The New York Times* (September 19, 2009), p. A17.
5. Susan J. Douglas, "Killing Granny with the Laziness Bias," *In These Times* (September 17, 2009), http://www.inthese times.com/main/article/4897/.
6. Mark Slouka, "A Quibble," *Harper's Magazine* (February 2009), p. 9.
7. Herbert, "The Scourge Persists," p. 17.

CHAPTER THREE

Zombie Language and the Politics of the Living Dead

In a robust democratic society, language and critical thought have a liberating function. At best, they work together to shatter illusions, strengthen the power of reason and critical judgment, and provide the codes and framing mechanisms for human beings to exercise a degree of self-determination while holding the throne of governmental, military, and economic power accountable. Language in such a society is engaged, critical, dialectical, historical, and creates the conditions for dialogue, thoughtfulness, and informed action. Such a language refuses to be co-opted in the service of marketing goods, personalities, and sleazy corporations. Needless to say, it is a language that is troubling and almost always threatening to the guardians of the status quo. As Toni Morrison points out in another context, language that is troubling has a way of reading and writing the world, that "can disturb the social oppression that functions like a coma on the population, a coma despots call peace...[that makes visible] the blood flow of war that hawks and profiteers thrill to."[1]

In authoritarian societies, language works to produce forms of historical and social amnesia, using the media, universities, and other sites of public pedagogy to cover the visual landscape with a coma-inducing ignorance. This political and moral coma allows the living dead to further experiment with those political mechanisms and social filters employed to freeze meaning, limit the discourses of freedom, and make certain ideas unspeakable, if not unthinkable. Tales of repression, cruelty, human suffering, and evil disappear from public memory, becoming invisible as politics works through a zombie-like language to make unjust and repressive power invisible. This type of coma-like amnesia seems to have become one of the defining features of the new American century. At the same time this language and the ideologies and modes of governing are always conditional, open to resistance, and capable of being challenged by new modes of discourse, understanding, and courage. One example can be seen in the ongoing resistance emerging in Iran against the state's use of power to extend its ever-increasing restrictions on the new media and Internet to curb the power of the living and vital language of dissent. It can also be seen in the rewriting of history textbooks by right-wing extremists who control the Texas State Board of Education. In their attempt to whitewash history, they have replaced the word capitalism with free-enterprise system, rejected the separation of church and state as a constitutional principle, injected the importance of what they call biblical and pro-Confederate values, and replaced references to the slave trade with the more innocuous "Atlantic triangular trade," and redefined the Israeli-Palestinian conflict as a struggle driven by Islamic fundamentalism.[2]

Language that is coma producing always serves the interests of the living dead, becoming zombie-like in its ability to sap the meaning of any political and ethical substance. Such a language is suffocating, Orwellian in its hypocrisy, and death-dealing and cruel in the relationships it often produces and legitimates. For instance, as Michael Moore points out in his film *Capitalism: A Love Story*, a number of blue-chip companies take out insurance policies on their employees without telling them. Not only do such policies offer tax breaks for the rich, they also provide very lucrative sums of money for corporations when an employee dies. Irma Johnson found this out the hard way after her husband, Daniel, died of brain cancer. She discovered that the bank that had fired him received close to $4.5 million dollars in insurance proceeds.[3] She got nothing. The corporations refer to these lucrative and cruel schemes as "dead peasant policies." This is a discourse in which the living dead literally benefit from the deaths of their fired employees—zombie politics at its most transparent and morally repulsive.

At its best, language can invite us to think beyond the given and the realm of common sense, becoming a powerful force for unleashing the power of insight, imagination, and possibility. Yet we live at a time when language is often deployed by those with social, political, and economic resources that narrow its horizons, close down its appeal to truth claims, and empty content of any viable substance. When employed by those corrupted by power, language is often stripped of elements of critique, thoughtfulness, and compassion. Such a language cheapens public values, the notion of the common good, and increasingly appropriates all potential spaces for a viable politics through a debased appeal to self-interest, personal fears, money, and national security.

If successful, the language of oppression and cruelty becomes normalized, removed from the sphere of criticism and the culture of questioning. Such a language does more than normalize ignorance, illiteracy, and irrationality; it also produces a kind of psychic hardening and deep-rooted pathology in a society increasingly willing to eliminate the policies that enable the social bonds and protections necessary for a substantive democracy. This language of cruelty, a zombie-inspired discourse of sorts, has been given a new life within the last few decades as it has become the *lingua franca* of powerful American politicians, corporations, and many in the dominant media. And it is mobilized to both dismantle the liberating function of critical reason and to stifle criticisms of a society that appears to be adrift. Such a discourse turns hate-talk into a commodity and human suffering into a spectacle.

Rarely do we find a robust language at work in the corporate-mediated public domains that provides a sustained criticism of an imperial presidency, an economic system removed from all political and ethical constraints, a debased and debasing celebrity culture, a market-driven notion of consumerism that strips people of any other vestige of agency, an utter disregard for the lawlessness and inequality caused by casino capitalism, a permanent war economy, and a discourse of contempt aimed at those marginalized by poverty and race in America. While there are certainly criticisms of such practices and policies at work in American society, they are either marginalized, trivialized, or simply treated with disdain and viewed as irrelevant by those in power.

Flashpoints in a culture often signal the rise of this language of cruelty, suggesting ruptures in the democratic fabric of a country that speak to something foreboding in its present and future that is not merely disturbing but portends a new kind of evil, a gathering storm capable of ushering in a new kind of authoritarianism. Hurricane Katrina, declarations supporting torture by elected officials, bailouts for the rich and indifference for the poor, and millions of people sleeping on the street or in tents signal something new and despairing about American society. The story continues. For instance, in June 2005, Vice President Dick Cheney, in response to revelations of torture at Guantanamo, claimed that the prisoners in the detention camp inhabited something similar to Club Med. According to Cheney, "They're living in the tropics. They're well fed. They've got everything they could possibly want."[4]

What is most scandalous about this remark is not the sheer duplicity of the misrepresentation, or even the trivialization of human rights violations, but the attempt to silence or make disappear an ever-expanding narrative of extreme cruelty and pain inflicted on the bodies of those who have been forced to inhabit, without any legal rights, what would be more aptly called Club Torture. We know from a number of reports and from the leaked images of Abu Ghraib prison that combatants in various U.S. detention centers have been subjected to the most horrendous forms of torture, often severely injured and left to suffer with irreparable mental anguish. In other instances of torture and abuse, detainees "have been murdered."[5] But there is more at work in Cheney's comments than fabrications designed to promote certain convenient ideological illusions central to the new world order promoted by the Bush administration. There is also a hidden order of politics that suggests a certain psychic hardening of the culture, the triumph of a debased language and politics over any semblance of ethics and civic courage—clearly reinforced by the loss of a critical media, schools that actually teach young people to think critically, and those public spheres where viable public analyses can take place. This is a new register and expression of cruelty for the American empire because it now defines itself unapologetically and with great arrogance through its exercise of what could be appropriately called radical evil.

Evidence of this type of psychic hardening and moral depravity extends far beyond the more recently revealed torture memos, the media's embrace of Sarah Palin's talk about death panels, the gleeful expressions of racism that are back in fashion, the rise of hate-radio, and the triumphalist justifications for imperial power that fuel the language of the likes of Dick Cheney, Michael Savage, and Fox News. Even after President Obama condemned torture and made it illegal once again, those politicians and lawyers who supported torture and played a prominent role in both legitimating it and sanctioning it under the Bush administration refused to exhibit the slightest bit of self-reflection or remorse over their support for a state that tortures. For instance, in a revealing interview with Deborah Solomon of *The New York Times* at the end of November 2009, James Inhofe, a conservative Republican Senator from Oklahoma, stated that he did not think that the naval base at Guantanamo should be closed because it was "a real resource."[6] Inhofe then talked about Gitmo—this Gulag for the stateless roundly condemned all over the world—as if it were a vacation spot generously provided by the U.S. government for detainees, many of whom were legally but unjustly rendered as part of America's war on terror. What is even more astounding is that Inhofe seemed completely unwilling to entertain the overwhelming and substantial body of evidence now available as a matter of public record that proves that many of the detainees at Guantanamo were subjected by the American government to sexual abuse, human rights violations, and the systemic practice of torture. He states, without any irony intended:

> The people there are treated probably better than they are in the prisons in America. They have more doctors and medical practitioners per inmate. They're eating better than anyone has ever eaten before. . . . One of the big problems is they become obese when they get there because they've never eaten that good before.[7]

There is more than denial and ignorance at work in Inhofe's answer. It is also symptomatic of a society that is no longer capable of questioning itself, unraveling its ability to think critically and act in a morally responsible way. This is a society in which language has become so debased and corrupted by power that morality and truth claims are no longer open to examination, and the consequences spell catastrophe for democracy. In another interview, Solomon asked John Yoo, the former Justice Department lawyer and one of the architects of the torture memos, if he regretted writing the memos, which offered President Bush a legal rationale for ignoring domestic and international laws prohibiting torture.[8] Exhibiting a complete indifference to the moral issue at stake in justifying systemic torture, Yoo provided an answer not unlike those provided by Nazi war criminals prosecuted at the Nuremberg military tribunals in 1945. He stated: "No, I had to write them. It was my job. As a lawyer, I had a client. The client needed a legal question answered."[9]

More recently, it was widely reported in the dominant media that there are over 39 million people on food stamps, and 6 million of these people have no other source of income. Put another way, "About one in 50 Americans now lives in a household with a reported income that consists of nothing but a food-stamp card."[10] These figures become all the more tragic when we learn that one in four children are on food stamps. Surely such a story should move the American public to both question any society with this degree of inequality and move in some transformative way to address the needless suffering of millions of people. When the story was reported in *The New York Times*, it was largely descriptive, the language used was bloodless, sterile, lacking any sense of either urgency or suggesting the need for political action on the part of the American public. The one criticism in the article came from John Linder, a Georgia Republican and a ranking member of the House Panel on Welfare Policy. Displaying what can truly be called a zombie politics and language only fit for persuading the living dead, he criticized the food stamp program, arguing that "We're at risk of creating an entire class of people, a subset of people, just comfortable getting by living off the government."[11] Linder's use of language mimics the moral depravity we find in the words of hot-shot investment bankers who hand out billions in bonuses while millions are starving because of the financial markets' recklessness. For the bankers, bonuses are—as one CEO put it—a form of God's work. There is more at play here than ignorance; there is also a deep sense of scorn for any viable notion of the welfare state and the necessity of government to address in a profound way the needless suffering of those caught in the expanding network of systemic inequality, unemployment, and poverty.

This use of dead language, stripped of insight, ethics, and compassion, has now become commonplace in America and suggests that we have become a country with no interest in modes of governance that extend beyond the narrow and often ruthless interests of investment bankers, mega-corporations, the ultra-rich, the

Department of Defense, and casino capitalism. Linguistic appeals to present-day zombies erase any viable notion of the social, public sphere, and the common good. Rather than talk about the responsibilities of the welfare state and social safety nets for the millions of Americans in need, government and corporate spokespersons employ a language of bare life—devoid of compassion and respect for the other. This is a language that erases the social and all of the human bonds and conditions necessary to provide human relationships with joy, dignity, hope, justice, and a measure of moral and social responsibility. The realm of the social, the glue of public life and the common good, has been utterly privatized within this death-inspired language and cut off from the political, economic, and moral connections that give society any viable identity and meaning. As the language of war, finance, and markets drives politics, matters of ethics, social responsibility, thinking from the place of the other, and addressing the conditions under which it becomes possible to apprehend the suffering of others becomes not only difficult but is more often than not treated with contempt.

Zombie language, with its appeal to the living dead, erases the social as it privatizes it and can only imagine freedom through the narrow lens of self-interest, exchange values, and profit margins. Troubles are now privatized, resulting in "yet more loneliness and impotence, and indeed more uncertainty still."[12] Society in this view is a network of random connections and disconnections, tied to furthering the interests of competitive individuals and fueled by a rabid individualism. Zombie language is more than Orwellian in that it does not merely offer up illusions, it arrogantly celebrates those values, structures, institutions and modes of power that are on the side of death, the perpetuation of human suffering, and a world-view that cannot think beyond the maximizing pleasures of grotesque power, wealth, and privilege.

Cheney, Inhofe, Yoo, the heads of the commanding financial institutions, and too many others to name exhibit and legitimize the type of zombie language along with an unethical mode of behavior that is chilling in its moral transgressions and telling in its reflection of the political and moral corruption that has taken hold of American culture. But the cruelties and crimes that these individuals, corporations, and administrations produce as official policy through a language of the living dead could not have taken place if there were not a formative culture in place in the United States that in its silence and complicity supported and enabled such a discourse and its accompanying acts of barbarism and cruelty. Within such a culture, as Judith Butler reminds us, it becomes increasingly easy for human life to be sacrificed to an instrumental logic, a totalitarian view of authority, and a discourse of fear. Such a culture loses its moral compass, sanctions cruel polices that produce massive human suffering and disposability, and in the end becomes unable to entertain those norms or shared conditions that make human life possible, that apprehend the dignity of human life or offer the political and moral frameworks "to guard against injury and violence."[13] Under such circumstances, individual rights, protections, and civil liberties disappear as the most barbaric state-sanctioned practices are carried out with only minor opposition registered by the American people. Zombie language and its accompanying practices and policies are nourished by the egocentric politics of a rabid individualism, the punishing values of casino capitalism, and the harsh logic of privatization in which all problems are now shifted onto the shoulders of individuals, who have to bear the full burden of solving them. The culture of cruelty that emerges in this market-driven ideology and the language that legitimates it points not merely to the death of public values or to a society that is politically adrift, but more importantly to the unleashing of institutions, ideas, values, and social relations that may lead to the demise of democracy itself.

NOTES

1. Toni Morrison, "Peril," in Toni Morrison, ed., *Burn This Book* (New York: HarperCollins, 2009), pp. 1–2.
2. Jack McKinley, Jr., "Texas Conservatives Win Curriculum Change," *The New York Times* (March 12, 2010), p. A10.
3. L.M. Sixel, "'Dead Peasant' Policies," *Houston Chronicle* (January 7, 2010), http://michaelmoore.com/words/mike-in-the-news/dead-peasant-policies.
4. Agence France-Presse, "Cheney Says Detainees Are Well Treated," *The New York Times* (June 24, 2005), http://www.nytimes.com/2005/06/24/politics/24cheney.html?pagewanted=print.
5. Three reports are especially useful on this matter. See Laurel E. Fletcher and Eric Stover, *Guantánamo and Its Aftermath: U.S. Detention and Interrogation Practices and Their Impact on Former Detainees* (Berkeley: Human Rights Center and International Human Rights Law Clinic, 2008), http://ccrjustice.org/files/Report_GTMO_And_Its_Aftermath.pdf; International Committee of the Red Cross, *ICRC Report on the Treatment of Fourteen "High Value" Detainees*, pp. 1–30; and Center for Constitutional Rights, *Report on Torture and Cruel, Inhuman, and Degrading Treatment of Prisoners at Guantánamo Bay, Cuba* (Washington, DC: Center for Constitutional Rights, 2006), http://ccrjustice.org/files/Report_ReportOnTorture.pdf.
6. Deborah Solomon, "Global Warning: Questions for James Inhofe," *The New York Times* (November 29, 2009), p. MM16.
7. Ibid.
8. Deborah Solomon, "Power of Attorney: Questions for John Yoo," *The New York Times* (January 3, 2010), p. MM15.
9. Ibid.
10. Jason Deparle and Robert M. Gebeloff, "Living on Nothing but Food Stamps," *The New York Times* (January 3, 2010), http://www.nytimes.com/2010/01/03/us/03foodstamps.html.
11. Ibid.
12. Zygmunt Bauman, *Liquid Times: Living in an Age of Uncertainty* (London: Polity Press, 2007), p. 14.
13. Judith Butler, *Frames of War: When Is Life Grievable?* (Brooklyn, NY: Verso, 2009), p. 3.

CHAPTER FOUR

Everyday Violence and the Culture of Cruelty

Entertaining Democracy's Demise

Under the Bush administration, a seeping, sometimes galloping authoritarianism began to reach into every vestige of the culture, giving free rein to those anti-democratic forces in which religious, market, military, and political fundamentalism thrived, casting an ominous shadow over the fate of U.S. democracy. During the Bush-Cheney regime, power became an instrument of retribution connected to and fuelled by a repressive state, a kind of zombie state trading in human abuse, fear, and punishment.[1] A bullying rhetoric of war, a ruthless consolidation of economic forces, and an all-embracing, free-market apparatus and media-driven pedagogy of fear supported and sustained a distinct culture of cruelty and inequality in the United States.

In pointing to a culture of cruelty, I am not employing a form of leftist moralism that collapses matters of power and politics into the discourse of character. On the contrary, I think the notion of a culture of cruelty is useful in thinking through the convergence of everyday life and politics, of considering material relations of power—the disciplining of the body as an object of control—on the one hand, and the production of cultural meaning, especially the co-optation of popular culture to sanction official violence, on the other. The culture of cruelty is important for thinking through how life and death now converge in ways that fundamentally transform how we understand and imagine politics in the current historical moment—a moment when the most vital elements of the social safety net are being undermined by right-wing ideologues. What is it about a culture of cruelty that provides the conditions for many Americans to believe that government is the enemy of health care reform and health care reform should be turned over to corporate and market-driven interests, further depriving millions of an essential right? And while a weak version of the health care bill has passed, the living undead are vowing to undo the bill through upcoming elections.

Increasingly, many individuals and groups now find themselves living in a society that measures the worth of human life in terms of cost-benefit analyses. The central issue of life and politics is no longer about working to get ahead but struggling simply to survive. And many groups considered marginal because they are poor, unemployed, people of color, elderly, or young, have not just been excluded from "the American dream" but have become utterly redundant and disposable, waste products of a society that no longer considers them of any value.[2] How else to explain the zealousness with which social safety nets have been dismantled, the transition from welfare to workfare (offering little job training programs and no child care), and the now infamous acrimony over health care reform's failed public option? What accounts for the passage of laws that criminalize the conduct of millions of homeless people in the United States, often defining sleeping, sitting, soliciting, lying down, or loitering in public places as a criminal offense rather than a behavior in need of compassionate good will and public assistance? Or, for that matter, the expulsions, suspensions, segregation, class discrimination, and racism in the public schools as well as the more severe beatings, broken bones, and damaged lives endured by young people in the juvenile justice system?

Within this type of zombie politics, largely fuelled by a market fundamentalism—one that substitutes the power of the social state with the power of the corporate state and only values wealth, money, and consumers—there is a ruthless and hidden dimension of cruelty, one in which the powers of life and death are increasingly determined by punishing apparatuses, such as the criminal justice system for poor people of color and/or market forces that increasingly decide who may live and who may die.

The growing dominance of right-wing media forged in a pedagogy of hate has become a crucial element providing numerous platforms for a culture of cruelty and is fundamental to how we understand the role of education in a range of sites outside of traditional forms of schooling. This educational apparatus and mode of public pedagogy are central to analyzing not just how power is exercised, rewarded, and contested in a growing culture of cruelty, but also how particular identities, desires, and needs are mobilized in support of an overt racism, hostility toward immigrants, and utter disdain coupled with the threat of mob violence toward any political figure supportive of the social contract and the welfare state. Citizens are increasingly constructed through a language of contempt for all non-commercial public spheres and a chilling indifference to the plight of others that is increasingly expressed in vicious tirades against big government and almost any form of social protection, however necessary. There is a growing element of scorn on the part of the American public for those human beings caught in a web of misfortune, human suffering, dependency, and deprivation. As Barbara Ehrenreich observes, "The pattern is to curtail financing for services that might help the poor while ramping up law enforcement: starve school and public transportation budgets, then make truancy illegal. Shut down public housing, then make it a crime to be homeless. Be sure to harass street vendors when there are few other opportunities for employment. The experience of the poor, and especially poor minorities, comes to resemble that of a rat in a cage scrambling to avoid erratically administered electric shocks."[3]

A right-wing spin machine, influenced by haters like Rush Limbaugh, Glenn Beck, Michael Savage, and Ann Coulter endlessly spews out a toxic rhetoric in which all Muslims are defined as jihadists; the homeless are not victims of misfortune but lazy; blacks are not terrorized by a racist criminal justice system but are the main architects of a culture of criminality; the epidemic of obesity has nothing to do with corporations, big agriculture, and advertisers selling junk food but rather the result of "big" government giving people food stamps; the public sphere is largely for white people, and it is being threatened by immigrants and people of color, and so it goes. Glenn Beck, the alleged voice of the common man, appearing on the *Fox & Friends* morning show, calls President Obama a "racist" and accuses him of "having a deep-seated hatred for white people or the white culture."[4] Nationally syndicated radio host Rush Limbaugh unapologetically states that James Earl Ray, the confessed killer of Martin Luther King, Jr., should be given a posthumous Medal of Honor,[5] while his counterpart in right-wing hate, talk radio host Michael Savage, states on his show, "You know, when I see a woman walking around with a burqa, I see a Nazi. That's what I see—how do you like that?—a hateful Nazi who would like to cut your throat and kill your children."[6] He also claims that Obama is "surrounded by terrorists" and is "raping America." This is a variation of a crude theme established by Ann Coulter, who refers to Bill Clinton as a "very good rapist."[7] Even worse, Obama is a "neo-Marxist fascist dictator in the making" who plans to "force children into a paramilitary domestic army."[8] And this is just a small sampling of the kind of hate talk that permeates right-wing media. This could be dismissed as loony right-wing political theater if it were not for the low levels of civic literacy displayed by so many Americans who choose to believe and invest in this type of hate talk.[9] On the contrary, while it may be idiocy, it reveals, as I state throughout this book, a powerful set of political, economic, and educational forces at work in miseducating the American public while at the same time extending the culture of cruelty and the politics of the hyper-dead. One central task of any viable form of politics is to analyze the culture of cruelty and its overt and covert dimensions of violence, often parading as entertainment.

Underlying the culture of cruelty that reached its apogee during the Bush administration was the legalization of state violence, such that human suffering was now sanctioned by the law, which no longer served as a summons to justice. But if a legal culture emerged that made violence and human suffering socially acceptable, popular culture rendered such violence pleasurable by commodifying, aestheticizing, and spectacularizing it. Rather than being unspoken and unseen, violence in American life had become both visible in its pervasiveness and normalized as a central feature of dominant and popular culture. Americans had grown accustomed to luxuriating in a warm bath of cinematic blood, as young people and adults alike were seduced with commercial and military video games such as *Grand Theft Auto* and *America's Army*,[10] the television series *24* and its ongoing Bacchanalian fête of torture, the crude violence on display in World Wrestling Entertainment and Ultimate Fighting Championship, and an endless series of vigilante films such as *The Brave One* (2007), *Death Sentence* (2007), and *Harry Brown* (2010), in which the rule of law is suspended by the viscerally satisfying images of men and women seeking revenge as laudable killing machines—a nod to the permanent state of emergency and war in the United States. Symptomatically, there is the mindless glorification and aestheticization of brutal violence in the most celebrated Hollywood films, including many of Quentin Tarantino's films, especially *Death Proof* (2007), *Kill Bill 1 & 2* (2003, 2004), and *Inglourious Basterds* (2009). With the release of Tarantino's 2009 bloody war film, in fact, the press reported that Dianne Kruger, the co-star of *Inglourious Basterds*, claimed that she "loved being tortured by Brad Pitt [though] she was frustrated she didn't get an opportunity to get frisky with her co-star, but admits being beaten by Pitt was a satisfying experience."[11] This is more than the aestheticization of violence; it is the normalization and glorification of torture itself.

If Hollywood has made gratuitous violence the main staple of its endless parade of blockbuster films, television has tapped into the culture of cruelty in a way that was unimaginable before the attack on the United States on September 11, 2001. Prime-time television before the attacks had "fewer than four acts of torture" per year, but "now there are more than a hundred."[12] Moreover, the people who torture are no longer the villains but the heroes of prime-time television. The most celebrated is, of course, Jack Bauer, the tragic-ethical hero of the wildly popular Fox TV thriller *24*. Not only is torture the main thread of the plot, often presented "with gusto and no moral compunction,"[13] but Bauer is portrayed as a patriot rather than a depraved monster who tortures in order to protect American lives and national security. Torture in this scenario takes society's ultimate betrayal of human dignity and legitimates the pain and fear it produces as normal, all the while making a "moral sadist" a television celebrity.[14] The show, before its final season in 2010, had over

15 million viewers, and its glamorization of torture had proven so successful that it appears not only to have numbed the public's reaction to the horrors of torture, but it became so overwhelmingly influential among the U.S. military that the Pentagon sent Brigadier General Patrick Finnegan to California to meet with the producers of the show. "He told them that promoting illegal behaviour in the series...was having a damaging effect on young troops."[15] The pornographic glorification of gratuitous, sadistic violence is also on full display in the popular HBO television series *Dexter*, which portrays a serial killer as a sympathetic, even lovable character. The Starz television series *Spartacus: Blood and Sand* takes the aesthetic of blood and violence beyond what one might call the pornography of violence. This series, a version of *Fight Club* on steroids, has more in common with the ideology and mechanisms of the fascist spectacle—at once a celebration of a ruthless form of hyper-masculinity, Social Darwinism, and an investment in violence as the most important element of power and mediating force in shaping social relationships. Violence in this series is more than grotesque; it is morally bankrupt and embraces the spectacle to both entertain and provoke the most debased type of voyeurism.[16]

The celebration of hyper-violence and torture travels easily from fiction to real life with the emergence in the past few years of a proliferation of "bum fight" videos on the Internet "shot by young men and boys who are seen beating the homeless or who pay transients a few dollars to fight each other."[17] The culture of cruelty mimics cinematic violence as the agents of abuse both indulge in actual forms of violence and then further celebrate the barbarity by posting it on the Web, mimicking the desire for fame and recognition, while voyeuristically consuming their own violent cultural productions. The National Coalition for the Homeless claims that "On YouTube in July 2009, people have posted 85,900 videos with 'bum' in the title [and] 5,690 videos can be found with the title 'bum fight,' representing...an increase of 1,460 videos since April 2008."[18] Rather than problematize violence, popular culture increasingly normalizes it, often in ways that border on criminal intent. For instance, a recent issue of *Maxim*, a popular men's magazine, included "a blurb titled 'Hunt the Homeless' [focusing on] a coming 'hobo convention' in Iowa and says 'Kill one for fun. We're 87 percent sure it's legal.'"[19] In this context violence is not simply being transformed into an utterly distasteful form of adolescent entertainment or spectacularized to attract readers and boost profits, it becomes a powerful pedagogical force in the culture of cruelty by both aligning itself and becoming complicit with the very real surge of violence against the homeless, often committed by young men and teenage boys looking for a thrill.[20] Spurred on by the ever-reassuring presence of violence and dehumanization in the wider culture, these young "thrill offenders" now search out the homeless and "punch, kick, shoot or set afire people living on the streets, frequently killing them, simply for the sport of it, their victims all but invisible to society."[21] All of these elements of popular culture speak stylishly and sadistically to new ways in which to maximize the pleasure of violence, giving it its hip (if fascist) edginess.

Needless to say, neither violent video games and television series nor Hollywood films and the Internet (or, for that matter, popular culture) cause in any direct sense real-world violence and suffering, but they do not leave the real world behind, either. That is too simplistic. What they do achieve is the execution of a well-funded and highly seductive public pedagogical enterprise that sexualizes and stylizes representations of violence, investing them with an intense pleasure quotient. I don't believe it is an exaggeration to claim that the violence of screen culture entertains and cleanses young people of the burden of ethical considerations when they, for instance, play video games that enable them to "casually kill the simulated human beings whose world they control."[22] Hollywood films such as the *Saw* series offer up a form of torture porn in which the spectacle of the violence enhances not merely its attraction but offers young viewers a space where questions of ethics and responsibility are gleefully suspended, enabling them to evade their complicity in a culture of cruelty. No warnings appear on the labels of these violent videos and films suggesting that the line between catharsis and desensitization may become blurred, making it more difficult for them to raise questions about what it means "to live in a society that produces, markets, and supports such products."[23]

But these hyper-violent cultural products also form part of a corrupt pedagogical assemblage and cultural apparatus that makes it all the more difficult to recognize the hard realities of power and material violence at work through militarism, a winner-take-all economy marked by punishing inequalities, and a national security state that exhibits an utter disregard for human suffering. In this version of zombie politics, death is spectacularized in order to evade matters of politics and power—even the suffering of children, we must note, as when government officials reduce the lives of babies and young children lost in Iraq and Afghanistan to collateral damage. Tragically, the crime here is much more than symbolic.

The ideology of hardness and cruelty runs through American culture like an electric current, sapping the strength of social relations and individual character, moral compassion, and collective action, offering up crimes against humanity that become fodder for video games and spectacularized media infotainment, and constructing a culture of cruelty that promotes a "symbiosis of suffering and spectacle."[24] As Chris Hedges argues,

> Sadism is as much a part of popular culture as it is of corporate culture. It dominates pornography, runs…through reality television and trash-talk programs and is at the core of the compliant, corporate collective. Corporatism is about crushing the capacity for moral choice. And it has its logical fruition in Abu Ghraib, the wars in Iraq and Afghanistan, and our lack of compassion for the homeless, our poor, the mentally ill, the unemployed and the sick.[25]

Bailouts are not going to address the ways in which individual desires, values, and identities are endlessly produced in the service of a culture of cruelty and inequality. Power is not merely material, it is also symbolic and is distributed through a society in ways we have never seen before. No longer is education about schooling. It now functions through the educational force of the larger culture in the media, Internet, electronic media, and through a wide range of technologies and sites endlessly working to undo democratic values, compassion, and any viable notion of justice and its accompanying social relations. What this suggests is a redefinition of both literacy and education. We need as a society to educate students and others to be literate in multiple ways, to reclaim the high ground of civic courage, and to be able to name, engage, and transform those forms of public pedagogy that produce hate and cruelty as part of the discourse of common sense. Otherwise, democracy will lose the supportive institutions, social relations, and culture that make it not only possible but even thinkable.

NOTES

1. This is taken up in great detail in Henry A. Giroux, *Against the Terror of Neoliberalism* (Boulder: Paradigm, 2008) and Sheldon S. Wolin, *Democracy Incorporated: Managed Democracy and the Specter of Inverted Totalitarianism* (Princeton: Princeton University Press, 2008).
2. Zygmunt Bauman, *Wasted Lives* (London: Polity Press, 2004).
3. Barbara Ehrenreich, "Is It Now a Crime to Be Poor?," *The New York Times* (August 9, 2009), p. wk9.
4. David Bauder, "Fox's Glenn Beck: President Obama Is a Racist," *Associated Press* (July 28, 2009), http://www.google.com/hostednews/ap/article/ALeqM5imGTdQH8JbOAWo_yKxNHpAMTCq_gD99N03TG0.
5. Limbaugh cited in Casey Gane-McCalla, "Top 10 Racist Limbaugh Quotes," *NewsOne* (October 20, 2008), http://newsone.com/obama/top-10-racist-limbaugh-quotes/.
6. Savage quoted in *Thinkers and Jokers* (July 2, 2007), http://thinkersandjokers.com/thinker.php?id=2688.
7. Coulter quoted in Don Hazen, "The Tall Blonde Woman in the Short Skirt with the Big Mouth," *AlterNet* (June 6, 2006), www.alternet.org/module/printversion/37162.
8. These quotes are taken from an excellent article by Eric Boehlert in which he criticizes the soft peddling that many in the press give to right-wing fanatics such as Michael Savage. See Eric Boehlert, "*The New Yorker* raises a toast to birther nut Michael Savage," *Media Matters for America* (August 3, 2009), http://mediamatters.org/print/columns/200908030038.
9. See Chris Hedges, "America the Illiterate," *CommonDreams* (November 10, 2008), www.commondreams.org/view/2008/11/10-6; Terrence McNally, "How Anti-Intellectualism Is Destroying America," *AlterNet* (August 15, 2008), www.alternet.org/module/printversion/95109.
10. For an excellent collection on military video games, see Nina B. Huntemann and Matthew Thomas Payne, eds., *Joystick Soldiers: The Politics of Play in Military Video Games* (New York: Routledge, 2010).
11. Arts and Entertainment, "Torture Will Just Have to Do," *The Hamilton Spectator* (August 12,

2009), p. Go 3.

12. Jane Mayer, "Whatever It Takes: The Politics of the Man Behind *24*," *The New Yorker* (February 26, 2007), p. 68.

13. Alessandra Stanley, "Suicide Bombers Strike, and America Is in Turmoil. Just Another Day in the Life of Jack Bauer," *The New York Times* (January 12, 2007), p. B1.

14. See Judith Butler, *Frames of War: When Is Life Grievable?* (New York and London: Verso, 2009); and Slavoj Zizek, "The Depraved Heroes of *24* Are the Himmlers of Hollywood," *The Guardian* (January 10, 2006), http://www.guardian.co.uk/media/2006/jan/10/usnews.comment.

15. Faiz Shaker, "U.S. Military: Television Series '24' Is Promoting Torture in the Ranks," *Think Progress* (February 3, 2007), http://thinkprogress.org/2007/02/13/torture-on-24/.

16. The aesthetics of the body and violence is taken up in Okwui Enwezor, "The Body in Question," *Third Text* (Summer 1995), pp. 67–70.

17. Eric Lichtblau, "Attacks on Homeless Bring Push on Hate Crime Laws," *The New York Times* (August 8, 2009), p. A1.

18. National Coalition for the Homeless, *Hate, Violence, and Death on Main Street, 2008* (Washington, D. C., National Coalition of the Homeless, 2009), http://www.national homeless.org/publications/hatecrimes/hate_report_2008.pdf, p. 34.

19. Lichtblau, "Attacks on Homeless Bring Push on Hate Crime Laws."

20. National Coalition for the Homeless, *Hate, Violence, and Death on Main Street, 2008*.

21. Lichtblau, "Attacks on Homeless Bring Push on Hate Crime Laws."

22. Mark Slouka, "Dehumanized: When Math and Science Rule the School," *Harper's Magazine* (September 5, 2009), p. 40.

23. Ibid.

24. Mark Reinhardt and Holly Edwards, "Traffic in Pain," in Mark Reinhardt and Holly Edwards, eds. *Beautiful Suffering* (Chicago: University of Chicago Press, 2006), p. 9.

25. Chris Hedges, "America Is in Need of Moral Bailout," *Truthdig* (March 23, 2009), http://www.truthdig.com/report/item/20090323_america_is_in_need_of_a_moral_bailout/.

Market-Driven Hysteria
and the Politics of Death

If we take seriously the ideology, arguments, and values now emanating from the right wing of the Republican Party, there is no room in the United States for a democracy in which the obligations of citizenship, compassion, and collective security outweigh the demands of what might be called totalizing market-driven society, that is, a society that is utterly deregulated, privatized, commodified, and largely controlled by the ultra-rich and a handful of mega-corporations. In such a society, there is a shift in power from government to markets and the emergence of a more intensified political economy organized around three principal concerns: deregulated markets, commodification, and disposability. In spite of the current failure of this system, right-wing Republicans and their allies are more than willing to embrace a system that erases all vestiges of the public good, turning citizens into consumers, while privatizing and commodifying every aspect of the social order—all the while threatening the lives, health, and livelihoods of millions of working-class and middle-class people.

If we listen to shock jocks on right-wing talk radio and an increasing number of their ilk in other media-driven spheres, casino capitalism is not only sexy, it provides an argument against the very notion of politics itself and the power of the government to intervene and protect its citizens from the ravages of nature, corrupt institutions, and an unregulated market. In this discourse, largely buttressed through an appeal to fear and the use of outright lies, free-market capitalism assumes an almost biblical status as an argument against the power of government to protect its citizens from misfortune and the random blows of fate by providing the most basic rights and levels of collective security and protection. Politics in this scenario is left to the fate of markets and the financial hyper-dead, while everyone else has to look out for themselves, bereft of any social protections or collective help from broader social spheres.

Before he died, President Franklin Delano Roosevelt advocated precisely for such rights, which he called a "second bill of rights," and which included the right "of every family to a decent home. The right to adequate medical care and the opportunity to achieve and enjoy good health. The right to adequate protection from the economic fears of old age, sickness, accident and unemployment. The right to a good education."[1] That is, those social and economic rights that provide a secure foundation for people to live with dignity and be free to become critical and engaged citizens, capable of both expanding their own sense of agency and freedom while being able to work with others to fulfill the demands of an aspiring democracy.

But in the truncated notion of freedom espoused by the right-wing extremists of casino capitalism, democracy is a deficit, if not a pathology, and freedom is reduced to the narrow logic of an almost rabid focus on self-interest. As I pointed out in the Introduction, this is a truncated version of freedom, defined largely as freedom from constraint—a freedom which when not properly exercised or balanced loses its connection to those obligations that tie people to values, issues, and institutions that affirm "the existence of a common good or a public purpose."[2] Freedom here operates according to a calculated deficit that reduces agency to a regressive infantilism, or what Leo Lowenthal called "the atomization of the individual," terrorized by other human beings, and reduced to "living in a state of stupor, in a moral coma."[3] This type of depoliticizing inward thinking, with its disavowal of the obligations of social responsibility and its outright disdain for those who are disadvantaged by virtue of being poor, young, or elderly, does more than fuel the harsh, militarized, and hyper-masculine logic of reality television and extreme sports. It also elevates death over life, selfishness over compassion, and economics over politics. But more so, it produces a kind of dysfunctional silence in the culture in the face of massive hardship and suffering, wiping out society's collective memories of moral decency.

There is more than moral indifference and political cynicism at work here. There is also a culture in which there is not much room for ideals, a culture that now considers public welfare a pathology, and responsibility solely a privatized and individual matter. Under this form of zombie politics and mode of casino capitalism, people become invested in their own survival, narrowly focused on their own interests, all the while confirming their regression into a Social Darwinism echoed daily on reality TV. This is a politics of disinvestment in public life, democracy, and the common good. Hence, it is not surprising that we hear nothing from the faux populists Glenn Beck, Rush Limbaugh, Bill O'Reilly and other cheerleaders for an unchecked capitalism about a market-driven landscape filled with desolate communities, gutted public services, and weakened labor unions. Nor do they say anything about a free-market system that in its greed, cruelty, corruption, and iniquitous power relations creates the conditions responsible for 40 million impoverished people (many living in their cars or the ever-growing tent cities), and 46 million Americans, until recently, living without health insurance—one result of which, according to a Harvard University study, has been the needless deaths of 45,000 people every year.[4] Nor do they register any alarm over a system that, according to a recent study released by the Johns Hopkins Children's Center, claims that "lack of adequate health care may have contributed to the deaths of some 17,000 U.S. children over the past two decades."[5] What do they have to say about a deregulated market system with its corrupt financial institutions shipping jobs abroad, swindling people out of their homes, and gutting the manufacturing base of U.S. industry? What do they have to say about a political system largely controlled by corporate lobbyists? Or insurance companies that pay employees bonuses when they maintain a high level of rejections for procedures that can save people's lives. Not much. All they see amid this growing landscape of human suffering and despair is the specter of socialism, which amounts to any government-sponsored program designed to offer collective insurance in the face of misfortune and promote the public good.

For many conservatives and right-wing extremists, a market-driven society represents more than a tirade against "big government." It constitutes a new kind of politics that privileges exchange values and quick profits over all non-commodified values, resists all forms of government intervention (except when it benefits the rich and powerful and the defense industry), celebrates excessive individualism, and consolidates the power of the rich along with powerful corporations—currently coded as mammoth financial institutions such as the insurance companies, pharmaceutical companies, and big banks. Moreover, the ability of this previously devalued market-driven system to endlessly come back to life is truly astonishing. How can the Dick Armeys of the world be featured in *The New York Times* as if their ideology and ruthlessness is worthy of a major news story? How is it that an endless number of ex and current politicians who are wedded at the hip to corporate interests can be taken seriously as spokespersons for the larger public?

As the fog of social and historical amnesia rolls over the media and the country in general, it does so in spite of the financial tsunami unleashed in 2008, the debacle following Hurricane Katrina, the Gulf oil crisis, and the in-your-face payout of big bonuses by institutions that were bailed out by the government. Clearly, market fundamentalism is alive and well in the United States, suggesting that it also works hard through the related modalities of education and seduction to induce the public to conform to the narrow dictates, values, and dreams of totalizing market society, regardless of how disruptive it is of their lives. Shouting against the evils of big government does little to register or make visible the power of big corporations or a government that serves corporate rather than democratic needs. Even as an ecological disaster looms along the Gulf Coast, there seems to be little analysis of how then Vice President Dick Cheney secretly convened the oil companies in order to set the standards for energy policy in the United States, setting the stage for eventual disasters such as the recent deep-sea oil leak in the Gulf that could have been prevented with proper government oversight. Nor is there any public outrage of how casino capitalism's most treasured formula of short-term investments for quick profits ignores the possibility of deadly social costs, especially regrettable as BP devoted little time to creating contingent plans in the event that one of its offshore oil wells failed, which, of course, it did. Such an investment would have cut into quick profits, and now billions will be spent, most likely taxpayers' money, to fix the ecological and human damage done along one of the most beautiful coastlines in America.

What is unique and particularly disturbing about this hyper-market-driven notion of economics is that it makes undemocratic modes of education central to its politics and employs a mode of pedagogy aimed at displacing and shutting down all vestiges of the public sphere that cannot be commodified, privatized, and commercialized. Consumers are in and citizens are out. Fear-mongering and lying are the discourses of choice, while dialogue and thoughtfulness are considered weakness. To a greater extent than at any other point in liberal modernity, this regime of Economic Darwinism now extends economic rationality "to formerly noneconomic domains [shaping] individual conduct, or more precisely, [prescribing] the citizen-subject of the neoliberal order."[6] Most crucially, this struggle over the construction of the market-driven consumer-subject, especially as it applies to young people, is by and large waged outside of formal educational institutions, in pedagogical sites and spaces that are generally privatized and extend from the traditional and new media to conservative-funded think tanks and private schools.[7] As corporate-controlled spheres and commodity markets assume a commanding role educating young and old alike, pedagogy is redefined as a tool of commerce aggressively promoting the commodification of young people and the destruction of non-commodified public spaces and institutions. How else to explain that it is almost impossible to read about educational reform in the dominant media except as a tool to educate people for the workforce? In other words, education is a form of commerce and nothing more. Education for democracy today sounds a lot like the idea that health care for everyone is socialism. Clearly, what we are witnessing here is not just the rise of political theater or media-driven spectacle in American society but a populism that harbors a deep disdain for democracy and no longer understands how to define itself outside of the imperatives of capital accumulation, shopping, and the willingness to view more and more individuals and groups as simply disposable, waste products no longer worthy of the blessings of consumption.

As moral and ethical considerations are decoupled from the calculating logic and consequences of all economic activity, the horrendous human toll in suffering and hardship being visited upon all segments of the American population is lost in the endless outburst of anger, if not hysteria, promoted by right-wing extremists shouting for a return to the good old days when financial institutions and money markets set policy, eventually ushering in one of the most serious economic crises this country has ever faced. As the values of human solidarity, community, friendship, and love are once again subordinated to the notion that only markets can give people what they want, the culture of fear and cruelty grows in proportion to the angry protests, the threat of violence, and the unapologetic racism aimed at the Obama administration. In part, this is exemplified in not only the endless public pronouncements that make a market society and democracy synonymous but also in the ongoing celebration, in spite of the near collapse of the mortgage sector, of the excesses of the new Gilded Age. Like those reanimated corpses that endlessly return in such classic zombie films as *Dawn of the Dead*, right-wing Republicans and Democrats are back shouting from every conceivable platform to demolish any vestige of reform that relies on "big government." The right-wing infatuation with the word "death," as in the fictitious claim about Obama's death panels, is telling—more a projection of their own politics than a serious critique of health care reform legislation. Despite a change in U.S. political leadership, these forces, if left unchecked, will continue to promote and fight for a transformation of democratic governance and citizenship until they are both completely destroyed.

As democracy is increasingly reduced to an empty shell and the rise of a corporate and punishing state looms heavily on the twenty-first-century horizon, the market-driven principles of deregulation, radical individualism, and privatization penetrate all aspects of daily life. Such market-driven values and their accompanying power-shaping institutions now profoundly influence the very nature of how Americans think, act, and desire. All of which are increasingly wedded to the epicenter of a grotesque consumer culture, whose underside is a heartless indifference to the suffering and hardship of the millions of people without jobs, homes, child care, and, increasingly, hope. The current fight against immigration and real educational reform is not really just about fixing a terribly iniquitous and broken system. It is a struggle against the prospect of a better future for young people, the poor, the excluded, and those struggling to stay alive in America. What are we to make of an ideology that moves from dismantling the welfare state to embracing the punishing state, an ideology that increasingly turns its back on those individuals for whom the prisons are now deputized as the only welfare institutions left in America, or, if they are lucky, who find themselves in one of the emerging tent cities found under bridges and located in other invisible landscapes—used in the past to get rid of waste products, but now used to dump poor working-class and middle-class families.

Where is this hysteria going, given that we now have in office an administration that refuses to fight for the ideals it campaigned on? We get a glimpse of where it is going in the tirades let loose recently by people like Sarah Palin, a dumber-than-dumb version of Ayn Rand, and Representative Michele Bachmann, Republican of Minnesota who. when she is not calling for members of Congress to be investigated for their communist sympathies, is railing against Obama's socialism. In leading crowds in Washington, DC, with the chant, "kill the bill," Bachmann displayed not simply an angry protest against health care reform. On the contrary, there is a much broader notion of politics at stake here, one in which she and others are protesting for an utterly privatized and commodified society where corporations and markets define politics while matters of life and death are removed from ethical considerations, increasingly subject to cost-benefit analyses and the calculations of potential profit margins. In this scenario, each individual is on his or her own in confronting the many systemic problems facing American society, each of us responsible for our own fate, even when facing systemic problems that cannot be solved by isolated individuals. This politics of hysteria and ruthlessness that is now on full display in America is not just an attack on the social state, big government, the public sphere, and the common good but on the very essence of politics and democracy. This is truly a politics of the hyper-dead, a zombie politics that celebrates death over life.

NOTES

1. For an excerpt of Roosevelt's call for a second bill of rights, see Bill Moyers, "Interview with James Galbraith," *Bill Moyers Journal* (October 30, 2009), http://www.pbs.org/moyers/journal/10302009/transcript4.html.
2. Ibid.
3. Leo Lowenthal, "Atomization of Man," *False Prophets: Studies in Authoritarianism* (New Brunswick, NJ: Transaction Books, 1987), p. 182.
4. U.S. Census Bureau Press Release, "Income, Poverty and Health Insurance Coverage in the United States: 2008," U.S. Department of Commerce, Washington, DC (September 10, 2009), http://www.census.gov/Press-Release/www/releases/archives/income_wealth/014227.html; Paul Klayman, "Harvard Study: 45,000 People Die Every Year," Institute for Southern Studies (September 18, 2009), http://www.southernstudies.org/2009/09/uninsured-die-every-year.html.

5. Editorial, "Lack of Health Care Led to 17,000 US Child Deaths," *Agence France-Presse* (October 29, 2009), www.truth.org/1030099?print.

6. Wendy Brown, *Edgework: Critical Essays on Knowledge and Politics* (Princeton: Princeton University Press, 2005), p. 41.

7. For an excellent analysis of the control of corporate power on the media, see Robert W. McChesney, *The Political Economy of the Media* (New York: Monthly Review Press, 2008).

CHAPTER SIX

Torturing Children: Bush's Legacy and Democracy's Failure

Salvos from the Culture of Cruelty

Nowhere is there a more disturbing, if not horrifying, example of the relationship between a culture of cruelty and the zombie politics of irresponsibility than in the resounding silence that surrounds the torture of children under the presidency of George W. Bush—and the equal moral and political failure of the Obama administration to address and rectify the conditions that made it possible. But if we are to draw out the dark and hidden parameters of such crimes, they must be made visible so men and women can once again refuse to orphan the law, justice, and morality. How we deal with the issue of state terrorism and its complicity with the torture of children will determine not merely the conditions under which we are willing to live but whether we will live in a society in which moral responsibility disappears altogether and whether we will come to find ourselves living under either a democratic or authoritarian social order. This is not merely a political and ethical matter but also a matter of how we take seriously the task of educating ourselves more critically in the future.

We haven't always looked away. When Emmett Till's battered, brutalized, and broken 14-year-old body was open to public viewing in Chicago after he was murdered in Mississippi in 1955, his mother refused to have him interred in a closed casket. His mutilated and swollen head, his face disfigured and missing an eye, made him unrecognizable as the young, handsome boy he once was. The torture, humiliation, and pain this innocent African American youth endured at the hands of white racists was transformed into a sense of collective outrage and pain, and helped launch the Civil Rights movement. Torture when inflicted on children becomes indefensible. Even among those who believe that torture is a defensible practice to extract information, the case for inflicting pain and abuse upon children proves impossible to support. The image of young children being subjected to prolonged standing, handcuffed to the top of a cell door, doused with cold water, raped, and shocked with electrodes boggles the mind. These corrupting, degenerate, and despicable practices reveal the utter moral depravity underlying the rationales used to defend torture as a viable war tactic.

There is an undeniable pathological outcome when the issue of national security becomes more important than the survival of morality itself, resulting in some cases in the deaths of thousands of children—and with little public outrage. For instance, then Secretary of State Madeleine Albright, appearing on the national television program *60 Minutes* in 1996, was asked by Leslie Stahl for her reaction to the killing of half a million Iraqi children in five years as a result of the U.S. blockade. Stahl pointedly asked her, "We have heard that a half million children have died. I mean, that's more children than died in Hiroshima. And, you know, is the price worth it?" Albright replied, "I think this is a very hard choice, but the price—we think the price is worth it."[1] The comment was barely reported in the mainstream media and produced no outrage among the American public. As Rahul Mahajan points out, "The inference that Albright and the terrorists may have shared a common rationale—a belief that the deaths of thousands of innocents are a price worth paying to achieve one's political ends—does not seem to be one that can be made in the U.S. mass media."[2]

More recently, Michael Haas has argued that in spite of the ample evidence that the United States has both detained and abused what may be hundreds of children in Iraq, Afghanistan, and Guantanamo, there has been almost no public debate about the issue and precious few calls for prosecuting those responsible for the torture. He writes:

> The mistreatment of children is something not so funny that has been neglected on the road to investigations of and calls for prosecution of those responsible for torture. George W. Bush has never been asked about the abuse of children in American-run prisons in the "war on terror." It is high time for Bush and others to be held accountable for what is arguably the most egregious of all their war crimes—the abuse and death of children, who should never have been arrested in the first place. The best kept secret of Bush's war crimes is that thousands of children have been imprisoned, tortured, and otherwise denied rights under the Geneva Conventions and related international agreements. Yet both Congress and the media have strangely failed to identify the very existence of child prisoners as a war crime.[3]

While it is difficult to confirm how many children have actually been detained, sexually abused, and tortured by the Bush administration, there is ample evidence that such practices have taken place not only from the accounts of numerous journalists but also in a number of legal reports. One of the most profoundly disturbing and documented cases of the torture of a child in the custody of U.S. forces is that of Mohammed Jawad, who was captured in Afghanistan after he allegedly threw a hand grenade at a military vehicle that injured an Afghan interpreter and two U.S. soldiers. He was immediately arrested by the local Afghan police, who tortured him and consequently elicited a confession from him. An Afghan Attorney General, in a letter to the U.S. government, claimed that Jawad was 12 years old when captured, indicating that he was still in primary school, though other sources claim he was around 15 or 16.[4] Jawad denied the charges made against him by the Afghan police, claiming that "they tortured me. They beat me. They beat me a lot. One person told me, 'If you don't confess, they are going to kill you.' So, I told them anything they wanted to hear."[5]

On the basis of a confession obtained through torture, Jawad was turned over to U.S. forces and detained first at Bagram and later at Guantanamo. This child, caught in the wild zone of permanent war and illegal legalities, has spent more than six years as a detainee. Unfortunately, the Obama administration, even after admitting that Jawad had been tortured illegally, has asked the court to detain him so that it can decide whether or not it wants to bring a criminal charge against him. After a federal judge claimed the government's case was "riddled with holes," the Obama administration decided it would no longer consider Jawad a "military detainee but would be held for possible prosecution in American civilian courts."[6] This shameful decision takes place against any sense of reason or modicum of morality and justice.

Even Jawad's former military prosecutor, Lt. Col. Darrel Vandeveld, a Bronze Star recipient, has stated that there "is no credible evidence or legal basis" to continue his detention and that he does not represent a risk to anyone.[7] In an affidavit filed with the American Civil Liberties Union (ACLU), he claimed "that at least three other Afghans had been arrested for the crime and had subsequently confessed, casting considerable doubt on the claim that Mr. Jawad was solely responsible for the attack."[8] It gets worse: Vandeveld also pointed out that the confession obtained by the Afghan police and used as the cornerstone of the Bush administration's case against Jawad could not have been written by him because "Jawad was functionally illiterate and could not read or write [and] the statement was not even in his native language of Pashto."[9] The ACLU points out that "the written statement [that] allegedly contain[s] Mohammed's confession and thumbprint is in Farsi," which Jawad does not read, write, or speak.[10]

Vandeveld was so repulsed by the fact that all of the evidence used against Jawad was forcibly obtained through torture that he "first demanded that Jawad be released, then, when Bush officials refused, unsuccessfully demanded to be relieved of his duty to prosecute and then finally resigned."[11] Since resigning, he is now a key witness in Jawad's defense and works actively with the ACLU to get him released. As Bob Herbert has written, "There is no credible evidence against Jawad, and his torture-induced confession has rightly been ruled inadmissible by a military judge. But the administration does not feel that he has suffered enough."[12] And yet Jawad was the subject of egregious and repugnant acts of torture from the moment he was captured in Afghanistan and later turned over to American forces.

In a sworn affidavit, Colonel Vandeveld stated that Jawad had undergone extensive abuse at Bagram for approximately two months: "The abuse included the slapping of Mr. Jawad across the face while Mr. Jawad's head was covered with a hood, as well as Mr. Jawad's having been shoved down a stairwell while both hooded and shackled."[13] As soon as Jawad arrived at Bagram, the abuse began, with him being forced to pose for nude photographs and undergo a stripsearch in front of a number of witnesses. He was also blindfolded and hooded while interrogated and "told . . . to hold on to a water bottle that he believed was actually a bomb that could explode at any moment."[14] In addition, while in the custody of U.S. forces, he was subjected to severe abuse and torture. According to the ACLU:

> U.S. personnel subjected Mohammed to beatings, forced him into so-called "stress positions," forcibly hooded him, placed him in physical and linguistic isolation, pushed him down stairs, chained him to a wall for prolonged periods, and subjected him to threats including threats to kill him, and other intimidation. U.S. forces also subjected Mohammed to sleep deprivation; interrogators' notes indicate that Mohammed was so disoriented at one point that he did not know whether it was day or night. Mohammed was also intimidated, frightened and deeply disturbed by the sounds of screams from other prisoners and rumours of other prisoners being beaten to death.[15]

The specifics of the conditions at Bagram under which Jawad was confined as a child are spelled out in a military interrogator's report:

> While at the BCP (Bagram Collection Point) he described the isolation cell as a small room on the second floor made of wood....He stated that while he was held in the isolation cells, they kept him restrained in handcuffs and a hood over his head, also making him drink lots of water. He said the guards made him stand up and if he sat down, he would be beaten....[He] stated that he was made to stand to keep him from sleeping and said when he sat down the guards would open the cell door, grab him by the throat and stand him up. He said they would also kick him and make him fall over, as he was wearing leg shackles and was unable to take large steps. He said the guards would fasten his handcuffs to the isolation cell door so he would be unable to sit down....[He] said due to being kicked and beaten at the BCP, he experienced chest pains and difficulty with urination.[16]

The interrogations, abuse, and isolation daily proved so debilitating physically and mentally that Jawad told military personnel at Bagram that he was contemplating suicide. What must be kept in mind is that this victim of illegal abuse and torture was only a juvenile, still in his teens and not even old enough to vote in the United States. Unfortunately, the torture and abuse of this child continued as he was transferred to Guantanamo. Starved for three days before the trip, given only sips of water, he arrived in Cuba on February 3, 2003, and was subjected to physical and linguistic isolation for 30 days—the only human contact being with interrogators. In October 2003, he underwent another 30-day period of solitary confinement. The interrogators displayed a ruthlessness with this young boy that is hard to imagine, all in the absence of legal counsel for Jawad. For instance, "Military records from throughout 2003 indicate that Mohammed repeatedly cried and asked for his mother during interrogation. Upon information and belief, before one interrogation, Mohammed fainted, complained of dizziness and stomach pain, but was given an IV and forced to go through with the interrogation."[17] Driven to despair over his treatment, Jawad attempted suicide on December 25, 2003. Hints of such despair had been observed by one interrogator, who approached a military psychologist and asked that the "techniques being applied to Jawad should be temporarily halted because they were causing him to dissociate, to crack up without providing good information."[18]

These techniques were particularly severe and, as Meteor Blades points out, can cause "physical deterioration, panic, rage, loss of appetite, lethargy, paranoia, hallucinations, self-mutilation, cognitive dysfunction, disorientation and mental breakdowns, any of which, alone or in combination, can spur the detainee to give interrogators more information than he might otherwise surrender."[19] Not only did Army Lieutenant Colonel Diane M. Zeirhoffer, a licensed psychologist, refuse to stop the abuse, which she had ordered; she also—according to the testimony of Lieutenant Colonel Vandeveld—engaged in a psychological assessment not to "assist in identifying and treating any emotional or psychological disturbances Mr. Jawad might have been suffering from. It was instead conducted to assist the interrogators in extracting information from Mr. Jawad, even exploiting his mental vulnerabilities to do so. . . . From my perspective, this officer had employed his or her professional training and expertise in a profoundly unethical manner."[20]

This is an egregious example of how the war on terror, its reign of illegal legalities, and its supportive culture of cruelty transforms members of a profession who take an oath to "do no harm" into military thugs who use their professional skills in the service of CIA and military interrogations and detainee torture—even the almost unspeakable torture of juveniles. The abuse of Jawad, bordering on Gestapo-like sadism, continued after his attempted suicide. From May 7–20, 2004, he was subjected to what military interrogators called the "frequent flyer" program, which was a systemic regime of sleep disruption and deprivation. In order to disrupt his sleep cycle, Jawad, according to military records, "was moved between two different cells 112 times, on average every two hours and 50 minutes, day and night. Every time he was moved, he was shackled."[21] As a result of this abuse, "Mohammed's medical records indicate that significant health effects he suffered during this time include blood in his urine, bodily pain, and a weight loss of 10% from April 2004 to May 2004."[22] At a June 2008 military commission hearing, Jawad's U.S. military lawyer inquired as to why "someone in a position of authority. . . and not just the guards" was not being held accountable for Jawad's subjection to the "frequent flyer" program.[23] The government refused to supply any names or prosecute anyone involved in the program, citing their right to privacy, as if such a right overrides "allegations of torture or other cruel, inhuman or degrading treatment or punishment and the right of victims of human rights violations to remedy."[24]

The torture and abuse of the child detainee Mohammed Jawad continued up to about June 2, 2008, when he was "beaten, kicked, and pepper-sprayed while he was on the ground with his feet and hands in shackles, for allegedly not complying with guards' instructions. Fifteen days later, there were still visible marks consistent with physical abuse on his body, including his arms, knees, shoulder, forehead, and ribs."[25] How the Obama administration could possibly defend building a criminal case against Mohammed Jawad, given that he was under 18 years of age at the time of his arrest and had endured endless years of torture and abuse at the hands of the U.S. government, raises serious questions about the ethical and political integrity of this government and its alleged commitment to human rights.

The case against this young man was so weak that Judge Ellen Segal Huvelle has not only accused the government of "dragging [the case] out for no good reason," but also expressed alarm at how weak the government's case was, stating in a refusal to give them an extension to amass new evidence against Jawad, "You'd better go consult real quick with the powers that be, because this is a case that's been screaming at everybody for years. This case is an outrage to me. . . . I am not going to sit up here and wait for you to come up with new evidence at this late hour. . . . This case is in shambles."[26] On July 30, 2009, Judge Huvelle ordered the Obama administration to release Jawad by late August. She stated, "After this horrible, long, tortured history, I hope the government will succeed in getting him back home....Enough has been imposed on this young man to date."[27] *The New York Times* reported, in what can only be interpreted as another example of bad faith on the part of the Obama administration, that the Justice Department responded to Judge Huvelle's ruling by suggesting that "they were studying whether to file civilian criminal charges against Mr. Jawad. If they do, officials say, he could be transferred to the United States to face charges, instead of being sent to Afghanistan, where his lawyers say he would be released to his mother."[28] In August of 2009, Mohammed Jawad was flown from Cuba to Afghanistan and released to his family. The U.S. government claims the criminal investigation is still open, but the chance of such an investigation taking place is now unlikely.

Even more disturbing are statements by Jawad's defense lawyers claiming that the witnesses who may be used in bringing a criminal case against Jawad were paid by the government for their testimony. According to U.S. Marine Corps Major Eric Montalvo, one of Jawad's lawyers, all of the alleged witnesses "received some sort of U.S. government compensation, from shoes and a trip to the United States to $400 for cooperation, which is a princely sum in Afghanistan."[29] This type of moral deception and sleazy illegality is straight from the playbook of high-level Republican operatives in the Bush/Cheney administration. Moreover, this response goes to the heart of the contradiction between Obama as an iconic symbol of a more democratic and hopeful future and the reality of an administration that is capable of reproducing some of the worst policies of the Bush administration.

Jawad's case is about more than legal incompetence. It is also about the descent into the "dark side" of a zombie politics where a culture of cruelty reigns and the rule of law is on the side of the most frightening of antidemocratic practices, pointing to a society in which terror becomes as totalizing as the loss of any sense of ethical responsibility. Torture of this type, especially of a child, would appear to have more in common with the techniques used by the Gestapo, Pol Pot, the Pinochet thugs in Chile, and the military junta in Argentina in the 1970s rather than with the United States—or at least the democratic country the United States has historically claimed to be.

Notes

1. See, for example, Rahul Mahajan, "We Think the Price Is Worth It," *Fairness & Accuracy in Reporting* (November/December 2001), http://www.fair.org/index.php?page=1084.
2. Ibid.
3. Michael Haas, "Children, Unlamented Victims of Bush War Crimes," *FactPlatform* (May 4, 2009), http://www.factjo.com/Manbar_En/MemberDetails.aspx?Id=187; and Michael Haas, *George W. Bush, War Criminal?: The Bush Administration's Liability for 269 War Crimes* (Westport, CT: Praeger Publishers, 2009).
4. Will Mathews, "Government Seeks to Continue Detaining Mohammed Jawad at Guantánamo Despite Lack of Evidence," *CommonDreams.Org* (July 24, 2009), http://www.commondreams.org/pring/45088; and ACLU Petition for Writ of Habeas Corpus, "Amended Petition."
5. Cited in Andy Worthington, "The Case of Mohammed Jawad," *Counterpunch* (October 17, 2007), http://www.counterpunch.org/worthington1017200.html.
6. William Glaberson, "Government Might Allow U.S. Trial for Detainee," *The New York Times* (July 25, 2009), p. A14.
7. ACLU, "Mohammed Jawad—Habeas Corpus," *Safe and Free* (January 13, 2009), http://www.aclu.org/safefree/detention/38714res20090113.html.
8. ACLU Petition for Writ of Habeas Corpus, "Amended Petition for Writ of Habeas Corpus on Behalf of Mohammed Jawad," June 2009, http://www.aclu.org/pdfs/natsec/amended_jawad

_2009113.pdf. "Amended Petition."

9. Ibid.

10. Ibid.

11. Glenn Greenwald, "Mohammed Jawad and Obama's Efforts to Suspend Military Commissions," *Salon.com* (January 21, 2009), http://www.salon.com/opinion/greenwald/2009/01/21/Guantánamo/.

12. Bob Herbert, "How Long Is Enough?", *The New York Times* (June 30, 2009), p. A21.

13. Colonel Vandeveld's sworn affidavit is included in the ACLU Petition for Writ of Habeas Corpus, "Amended Petition."

14. Ibid.

15. Ibid.

16. Amnesty International, *United States of America—From Ill-Treatment to Unfair Trial: The Case of Mohammed Jawad, Child Enemy Combatant* (London: Amnesty International, 2008), pp. 12–13.

17. ACLU Petition for Writ of Habeas Corpus, "Amended Petition."

18. Meteor Blades, "Army Psychologist Pleads 'Fifth' in Case of Prisoner 900," *DailyKos* (August 14, 2008), http://www.dailykos.com/story/2008/8/14/202414/685/395/568118.

19. Ibid.

20. Colonel Vandeveld's sworn affidavit is included in the ACLU Petition for Writ of Habeas Corpus, "Amended Petition."

21. Amnesty International, *United States of America*, p. 20.

22. ACLU Petition for Writ of Habeas Corpus, "Amended Petition."

23. Amnesty International, *United States of America*, p. 31.

24. Ibid.

25. ACLU Petition for Writ of Habeas Corpus, "Amended Petition."

26. Cited in Jason Leopold, "Obama Administration Cooks Up New Legal Argument for Detaining Guantánamo Prisoner," *Truthout* (July 28, 2009), http://www.truthout.org/072809.

27. Valtin, "'So Ordered': U.S. to Release Mohammed Jawad After Six Years of False Imprisonment," *Daily Kos* (July 30, 2009), http://www.dailykos.com/story/2009/7/30/18119/5521.

28. William Glaberson, "Judge Orders Release of Young Detainee at Guantánamo," *The New York Times* (July 31, 2009), P. A14.

29. Cited in Daphine Eviatar, "Military Lawyer Claims US Paid Guantanamo Prosecution Witnesses," *The Washington Independent* (August 5, 2009), http://washingtonindependent.com/53655/gitmo-detainee-claims-u-s-paid-prosecution-witnesses.

SECTION II

Zombie Theater and the Spectacle of Illiteracy

CHAPTER SEVEN

The Spectacle of Illiteracy and the Crisis of Democracy

C. Wright Mills argued fifty years ago that one important measure of the demise of vibrant democracy and the corresponding impoverishment of political life can be found in the increasing inability of a society to translate private troubles to broader public issues.[1] This is an issue that both characterizes and threatens any viable notion of democracy in the United States in the current historical moment. In an alleged post-racist democracy, the image of the public sphere with its appeal to dialogue and shared responsibility has given way to the spectacle of unbridled intolerance, ignorance, seething private fears, unchecked anger, and the decoupling of reason from freedom. Increasingly, as witnessed in the utter disrespect and not-so-latent racism expressed by Joe Wilson, the Republican congressman from South Carolina, who shouted "You lie!" during President Obama's address on health care, the obligation to listen, respect the views of others, and engage in a literate exchange is increasingly reduced to the highly spectacularized embrace of an infantile emotionalism. This is an emotionalism that is made for television. It is perfectly suited for emptying the language of public life of all substantive content, reduced in the end to a playground for hawking commodities, promoting celebrity culture, and enacting the spectacle of right-wing fantasies fueled by the fear that the public sphere as an exclusive club for white male Christians is in danger of collapsing. For some critics, those who carry guns to rallies or claim Obama is a Muslim and not a bona fide citizen of the United States are simply representative of an extremist fringe that gets far more publicity from the mainstream media than they deserve. Of course this is understandable, given that the media's desire for balance and objective news is not just disengenuous but relinquishes any sense of ethical responsibility by failing to make a distinction between an informed argument and an unsubstantiated opinion. Witness the racist hysteria unleashed by so many Americans and the media over the building of an Islamic cultural center near Ground Zero.

The collapse of journalistic standards finds its counterpart in the rise of civic illiteracy. An African American president certainly makes the Rush Limbaughs of the world even more irrational than they already are, just as the lunatic fringe seems to be able to define itself only through a mode of thought whose first principle is to disclaim logic itself. But I think this dismissal is too easy. What this decline in civility, the emergence of mob behavior, and the utter blurring in the media between a truth and a lie suggest is that we have become one of the most illiterate nations on the planet. I don't mean illiterate in the sense of not being able to read, though we have far too many people who are functionally illiterate in a so-called advanced democracy, a point that writers such as Chris Hedges, Susan Jacoby, and the late Richard Hofstadter made clear in their informative books on the rise of anti-intellectualism in American life.[2] I am talking about a different species of ignorance and anti-intellectualism. Illiterate in this instance refers to the inability on the part of much of the American public to grasp private troubles and the meaning of the self in relation to larger public problems and social relations. It is a form of illiteracy that points less to the lack of technical skills and the absence of certain competencies than to a deficit in the realms of politics—one that subverts both critical thinking and the notion of literacy as both critical interpretation and the possibility of intervention in the world. This type of illiteracy is not only incapable of dealing with complex and contested questions, it is also an excuse for glorifying the principle of self-interest as a paradigm for understanding politics. This is a form of illiteracy marked by the inability to see outside of the realm of the privatized self, an illiteracy in which the act of translation withers, reduced to a relic of another age. The United States is a country that is increasingly defined by a civic deficit, a chronic and deadly form of civic illiteracy that points to the failure of both its educational system and the growing ability of anti-democratic forces to use the educational force of the culture to promote the new illiteracy. As this widespread illiteracy has come to dominate American culture, we have moved from a culture of questioning to a culture of shouting and in doing so have restaged politics and power in both unproductive and anti-democratic ways.

Think of the forces at work in the larger culture that work overtime to situate us within a privatized world of fantasy, spectacle, and resentment that is entirely removed from larger social problems and public concerns. For instance, corporate culture with its unrelenting commercials carpet-bombs our audio and visual fields with the message that the only viable way to define ourselves is to shop and consume in an orgy of private pursuits. Popular culture traps us in the privatized universe of celebrity culture, urging us to define ourselves through the often empty and trivialized and highly individualized interests of celebrities. Pharmaceutical companies urge us to deal with our problems, largely produced by economic and political forces out of our control, by taking a drug, one that will both chill us out and increase their profit margins. (This has now become an educational measure applied increasingly and indiscriminately to children in our schools.) Pop psychologists urge us to simply think positively, give each other hugs, and pull ourselves up by the bootstraps while also insisting that those who confront reality and its mix of complex social issues are, as Chris Hedges points out, defeatists, a negative force that inhibits "our inner essence and power."[3] There is also the culture of militarization, which permeates all aspects of our lives—from our classrooms and the screen culture of reality television to the barrage of violent video games and the blood letting in sports such as popular wrestling—endlessly at work in developing modes of masculinity that celebrate toughness, violence, cruelty, moral indifference, and misogyny.

All of these forces, whose educational influence should never be underestimated, constitute a new type of illiteracy, a kind of civic illiteracy in which it becomes increasingly impossible to connect the everyday problems that people face with larger social forces—thus depoliticizing their own sense of agency and making politics itself an empty gesture. Is it any wonder that politics is now mediated through a spectacle of anger, violence, humiliation, and rage that mimics the likes of *The Jerry Springer Show*? It is not that we have become a society of the spectacle—though that is partly true—but that we have fallen prey to a new kind of illiteracy in which the distinction between illusion and reality is lost, just as the ability to experience our feelings of discontent, and our fears of uncertainty are reduced to private troubles, paralyzing us in a sea of resentment waiting to be manipulated by extremists extending from religious fanatics to right-wing radio hosts. This is a prescription for a kind of rage that looks for easy answers, demands a heightened emotional release, and resents any attempts to think through the connection between our individual woes and any number of larger social forces. A short list of such forces would include an unchecked system of finance, the anti-democratic power of the corporate state, the rise of multinationals and the destruction of the manufacturing base, and the privatization of public schooling along with its devaluing of education as a public good. As the public collapses into the personal, the personal becomes "the only politics there is, the only politics with a tangible referent or emotional valence,"[4] the formative educational and political conditions that make a democracy possible begin to disappear. Under such circumstances, the language of the social is either devalued, pathologized, or ignored, and all dreams of the future are now modeled around the narcissistic, privatized, and self-indulgent needs of consumer and celebrity culture and the dictates of the allegedly free market. How else to explain the rage against big government but barely a peep against the rule of big corporations who increasingly control not only the government but almost every vital aspect of our lives from health care to the quality of our environment?

Stripped of its ethical and political importance, the public has been largely reduced to a space where private interests are displayed, and the social order increasingly mimics a giant *Dr. Phil* show where notions of the public register as simply a conglomeration of private woes, tasks, conversations, and problems. Most importantly, as the very idea of the social collapses into an utterly privatized discourse, everyday politics is decoupled from its democratic moorings, and it becomes more difficult for people to develop a vocabulary for understanding how private problems and public issues constitute the very lifeblood of a vibrant politics and democracy itself. This is worth repeating. Emptied of any substantial content, democracy appears imperiled as individuals are unable to translate their privately suffered misery into genuine public debate, social concerns, and collective action. This is a form of illiteracy that is no longer marginal to American society but is increasingly becoming one of its defining and more frightening features.

The raging narcissism that seems to shape every ad, film, television program, and appeal now mediated through the power of the corporate state and consumer society is not merely a clinical and individual problem. It is the basis for a new kind of mass illiteracy that is endlessly reproduced through the venues of a number of anti-democratic institutions and forces that eschew critical debate, self-reflection, critical analysis, and certainly modes of dissent that call the totality of a society into question. As American society becomes incapable of questioning itself, the new illiteracy parades as just its opposite. We are told that education is about learning how to take tests rather than learning how to think critically. We are told that anything that does not make us feel good is not worth bothering with. We are told that character is the only measure of how to judge people who are the victims of larger social forces that are mostly out of their control. When millions of people are unemployed, tossed out of their homes, homeless, or living in poverty, the language of character, pop psychology, consumerism, and celebrity culture are more than a diversion: they are fundamental to the misdirected anger, mob rule, and illiteracy that frames the screaming, racism, lack of civility, and often sheer and legitimate desperation.

Authoritarianism is often abetted by an inability of the public to grasp how questions of power, politics, history, and public consciousness are mediated at the interface of private issues and public concerns. The ability to translate private problems into social considerations is fundamental to what it means to reactivate political sensibilities and conceive of ourselves as critical citizens, engaged public intellectuals, and social agents. Just as an obsession with the private is at odds with a politics informed by public consciousness, it also burdens politics by stripping it of the kind of political imagination and collective hope necessary for a viable notion of meaning, hope, and political agency.

Civic literacy is about more than enlarging the realm of critique and affirming the social. It is also about public responsibility, the struggle over democratic public life, and the importance of critical education in a democratic society. The U.S. government is more than willing to invest billions in wars, lead the world in arms sales, and give trillions in tax cuts to the ultra-rich but barely acknowledges the need to invest in those educational and civic institutions—from schools to the arts to a massive jobs creation program—that enable individuals to be border crossers, capable of connecting the private and the public as part of a more vibrant understanding of politics, identity, agency, and governance. The new illiteracy is not the cause of our problems, which are deeply rooted in larger social, economic, and political forces that have marked the emergence of the corporate state, a deadly form of racism parading as color blindness, and a ruthless market fundamentalism since the 1970s, but it is a precondition for locking individuals into a system in which they are complicitous in their own exploitation, disposability, and potential death.

The new illiteracy is about more than not knowing how to read the book or the word; it is about not knowing how to read the world. The challenge it poses in a democracy is one of both learning how to reclaim literacy so as to be able to narrate oneself and the world from a position of agency. But it is also about unlearning those modes of learning that internalize modes of ignorance based on the concerted refusal to know, be self-reflective, and act with principled dignity. It is a problem as serious as any we have ever faced in the United States. At the core of any viable democratic politics is the ability to question the assumptions central to an imagined democracy. This is not merely a political issue but an educational issue, one that points to the need for modes of civic education that provide the knowledge and competencies for young and old alike to raise important questions about what education and literacy itself should accomplish in a democracy.[5] This is not an issue we can ignore too much longer.

NOTES

1. C. Wright Mills, *The Sociological Imagination* (New York: Oxford University Press, 1959). See also the brilliant Richard Sennett, *The Fall of Public Man* (New York: W.W. Norton, 1992).
2. Richard Hofstadter, *Anti-Intellectualism in American Life* (New York: Vintage, 1966); Susan Jacoby, *The Age of American Unreason* (New York: Vintage, 2009); Chris Hedges, *Empire of Illusion* (Toronto: Knopf Canada, 2009).

3. Chris Hedges, "Celebrity Culture and the Obama Brand," *Tikkun* (January/February 2010). http://www.tikkun.org/article.php/jan10_hedges

4. Jean Comaroff and John L. Comaroff, "Millennial Capitalism: First Thoughts on a Second Coming," *Public Culture* 12:2 (2000), pp. 305–306.

5. Zygmunt Bauman,"Introduction," *Society under Siege* (Malden, MA: Blackwell, 2002), p. 170.

CHAPTER EIGHT

Zombie Politics and the Challenge of Right-Wing Teaching Machines

Rethinking the Importance of the Powell Memo

Paul Krugman, the Nobel Prize-winning economist, echoing the feelings of many progressives, in 2009 wrote in *The New York Times* about how dismayed he was over the success that right-wing ideologues had in undercutting Obama's health care bill—watering it down to a shadow of what it could have been before it finally became law. He further indicated how unsettled he was by the ability of conservatives to mobilize enormous public support against almost any reform aimed at rolling back the economic, political, and social conditions that have created the economic recession and the legacy of enormous suffering and hardship for millions of Americans over the last thirty years.[1] Krugman is somewhat astonished that after almost three decades the political scene is still under the sway of what he calls the "zombie doctrine of Reaganism"—the notion that any action by government is bad, except when it benefits the military, corporations, and the rich. Clearly, for Krugman, zombie Reaganism appears once again to be shaping policies under the Obama regime.

And yet, updated neoliberal Reaganism with its hatred of the social state, its celebration of unbridled self-interest, its endless quest to privatize everything, and its unflinching support for the deregulation of the economic system eventually brought the country to economic near-collapse. It also produced enormous suffering for those who never benefited from the excesses of the second Gilded Age, especially unemployed and underemployed workers, the poor, disadvantaged minorities, and eventually large segments of the middle class. And yet zombie politics or casino capitalism is back fighting efforts to strengthen bank regulations, resisting caps on CEO bonuses, preventing climate control legislation, and refusing to limit military spending. Unlike other pundits, Krugman does not merely puzzle over how zombie politics can keep turning up on the political scene, a return not unlike the endless corpses who keep coming back to life in George Romero's 1968 classic film, *Night of the Living Dead* (think of Bill Kristol, who seems to be wrong about everything but just keeps coming back like a character in a Romero film). Krugman takes the reader beyond mere puzzlement and argues that a wacky and allegedly discredited right-wing politics is far from dead. In fact, Krugman argues that one of the great challenges of the current moment is to try to understand the conditions that have allowed it to once again shape American politics and culture, given the enormous problems, including the current recession, it has produced at all levels of American society in the last thirty years.

Part of the explanation for the enduring quality of such a destructive politics can be found in the lethal combination of money, power, and education that the right wing has had a stranglehold on since the early 1970s. Financial power plus an insightful understanding of the importance of cultural politics has allowed conservatives to use their influence to develop an institutional infrastructure and ideological apparatus to produce their own intellectuals, disseminate ideas, and eventually control most of the commanding heights and institutions in which knowledge is produced, circulated, and legitimated. This is not simply a story about the rise of mean-spirited buffoons such as Glenn Beck, Bill O'Reilly, and Michael Savage. Nor is it simply a story about the loss of language, a growing anti-intellectualism in the larger culture, or the spread of what some have called a new illiteracy endlessly being produced in popular culture. As important as these tendencies are, there is something more at stake here that points to a combination of power, money, and education in the service of creating an almost lethal restriction on what can be heard, said, learned, and debated in the public sphere. And one starting point for understanding this problem is what has been called the Powell Memo—released on August 23, 1971—authored by Lewis F. Powell, who would later be appointed to the Supreme Court of the United States. Powell sent the memo to the U.S. Chamber of Commerce with the title "Attack on the American Free Enterprise System."

This memo is important because it reveals the power that conservatives attributed to the political nature of education and the significance this view had in shaping the long-term strategy they put into place in the 1960s and 1970s to win an ideological war against liberal intellectuals, who argued for holding government and corporate power accountable as a precondition for extending and expanding the promise of an inclusive democracy. The current concerted assault on government and any other institutions not dominated by free-market principles represents the high point of a fifty-year strategy that was first put into place by conservative ideologues such as Frank Chodorov, the founder of the Intercollegiate Studies Institute; publisher and author William F. Buckley; former Nixon Treasury Secretary William Simon; and Michael Joyce, the former head of both the Olin Foundation and the Lynde and Harry Bradley Foundation. The Powell Memo is important because it is the most succinct statement, if not the founding document, for establishing a theoretical framework and political blueprint for the current assault on any vestige of democratic public life that does not subordinate itself to the logic of the allegedly free market.

Initially, Powell identified the American college campus "as the single most dynamic source" for producing and housing intellectuals "who are unsympathetic to the [free] enterprise system."[2] He was particularly concerned about the lack of conservatives in social sciences faculties and urged his supporters to use an appeal to academic freedom as an opportunity to argue for "political balance" on university campuses. Powell recognized that one crucial strategy in changing the political composition of higher education was to convince university administrators and boards of trustees that the most fundamental problem facing universities was "the imbalance of many faculties."[3] Powell insisted that "the basic concepts of balance, fairness and truth are difficult to resist, if properly presented to boards of trustees, by writing and speaking, and by appeals to alumni associations and groups."[4] But Powell was not only concerned about what he perceived as the need to enlist higher education as a bastion of conservative, free-market ideology.

The Powell Memo was designed to develop a broad-based strategy both to counter dissent and develop a material and ideological infrastructure with the capability to transform the American public consciousness through a conservative pedagogical commitment to reproduce the knowledge, values, ideology, and social relations of the corporate state. For Powell, the war against liberalism and a substantive democracy was primarily a pedagogical *and* political struggle designed both to win the hearts and minds of the general public and to build a power base capable of eliminating those public spaces, spheres, and institutions that nourish and sustain what Samuel Huntington would later call (in a 1975 study on the "governability of democracies" by the Trilateral Commission) an "excess of democracy."[5] Central to such efforts was Powell's insistence that conservatives nourish a new generation of scholars who would inhabit the university and function as public intellectuals actively shaping the direction of policy issues. He also advocated the creation of a conservative speaker's bureau, staffed by scholars capable of evaluating "textbooks, especially in economics, political science and sociology."[6] In addition, he advocated organizing a corps of conservative public intellectuals who would monitor the dominant media, publish their own scholarly journals, books, and pamphlets, and invest in advertising campaigns to enlighten the American people on conservative issues and policies.

The Powell Memo, while not the only influence, played an important role in convincing a "cadre of ultraconservative and self-mythologizing millionaires bent on rescuing the country from the hideous grasp of Satanic liberalism"[7] to match their ideological fervor with their pocketbooks by "disbursing the collective sum of roughly $3 billion over a period of thirty years in order to build a network of public intellectuals, think tanks, advocacy groups, foundations, media outlets, and powerful lobbying interests."[8] As Dave Johnson points out, the initial effort was slow but effective:

> In 1973, in response to the Powell memo, Joseph Coors and Christian-right leader Paul Weyrich founded the Heritage Foundation. Coors told Lee Edwards, historian of the Heritage Foundation, that the Powell memo persuaded him that American business was "ignoring a crisis." In response, Coors decided to help provide the seed funding for the creation of what was to become the Heritage Foundation, giving $250,000. Subsequently, the Olin Foundation, under the direction of its president, former Treasury Secretary William Simon (author of the influential 1979 book *A Time for Truth*), began funding similar organizations in concert with "the Four Sisters"—Richard Mellon Scaife's various foundations, the Lynde and Harry Bradley Foundation, the Olin Foundation and the Smith Richardson Foundation—along with Coors's foundations, foundations associated with the Koch oil family, and a group of large corporations.[9]

The most powerful members of this group were Joseph Coors in Denver, Richard Mellon Scaife in Pittsburgh, John Olin in New York City, David and Charles Koch in Wichita, the Smith Richardson family in North Carolina, and Harry Bradley in Milwaukee—all of whom agreed to finance a number of right-wing think tanks, which over the past thirty years have come to include the Lynde and Harry Bradley Foundation, the Koch Foundation, the Castle Rock Foundation, and the Sarah Scaife Foundation. This formidable alliance of far-right-wing foundations deployed their resources in building and strategically linking "an impressive array of almost 500 think tanks, centers, institutes and concerned citizens groups both within and outside of the academy. . . . A small sampling of these entities includes the Cato Institute, the Heritage Foundation, the American Enterprise Institute, the Manhattan Institute, the Hoover Institution, the Claremont Institute, the American Council of Trustees and Alumni, [the] Middle East Forum, Accuracy in Media, and the National Association of Scholars, as well as [David] Horowitz's Center for the Study of Popular Culture."[10]

For several decades, right-wing extremists have labored to put into place an ultra-conservative re-education machine—an apparatus for producing and disseminating a public pedagogy in which everything tainted with the stamp of liberal origin and the word "public" would be contested and destroyed. Commenting on the rise of this vast right-wing propaganda machine organized to promote the idea that democracy needs less critical thought and more citizens whose only role is to consume, well-known author Lewis Lapham writes:

> The quickening construction of Santa's workshops outside the walls of government and the academy resulted in the increased production of pamphlets, histories, monographs, and background briefings intended to bring about the ruin of the liberal ideal in all its institutionalized forms—the demonization of the liberal press, the disparagement of liberal sentiment, the destruction of liberal education—and by the time Ronald Reagan arrived in triumph at the White House in 1980 the assembly lines were operating at full capacity.[11]

Any attempt to understand and engage the current right-wing assault on all vestiges of the social contract, the social state, and democracy itself will have to begin with challenging this massive infrastructure, which functions as one of the most powerful teaching machines we have seen in the United States, a teaching machine that produces a culture that is increasingly poisonous and detrimental not just to liberalism but to the formative culture that makes an aspiring democracy possible. The presence of this ideological infrastructure extending from the media to other sites of popular education suggests the need for a new kind of debate, one that is not limited to isolated issues such as health care, but is more broad based and fundamental, a debate about how power, inequality, and money constrict the educational, economic, and political conditions that make democracy possible. The screaming harpies and mindless anti-public "intellectuals" who dominate the media today are not the problem: it is the conditions that give rise to the institutions that put them in place, finance them, and drown out other voices. What must be clear is that this threat to creating a critically informed citizenry is not merely about a crisis of communication and language but also about the ways in which money and power create the educational conditions that make a mockery out of debate while hijacking any trace of democracy.

NOTES

1. Paul Krugman, "All the President's Zombies," *The New York Times* (August 24, 2009), p. A17.
2. Lewis F. Powell, Jr., "The Powell Memo," *ReclaimDemocracy.org* (August 23, 1971), http://reclaimdemocracy.org/corporate_accountability/powell_memo_lewis.html.
3. Ibid.
4. Ibid.
5. See Michael P. Crozier, Samuel. J. Huntington, and J. Watanuki, *The Crisis of Democracy: Report on the Governability of Democracies to the Trilateral Commission* (New York: New York University Press, 1975).
6. Powell, "The Powell Memo."
7. Lewis H. Lapham, "Tentacles of Rage—The Republican Propaganda Mill, a Brief History,"

Harper's Magazine (September 2004), p. 32.

8. Dave Johnson, "Who's Behind the Attack on Liberal Professors?" *History News Network* (February 10, 2005), http://hnn.us/articles/printfriendly/1244.html.

9. Ibid.

10. Alan Jones, "Connecting the Dots," *Inside Higher Ed* (June 16, 2006), http://insidehighered.com/views/2006/06/16/jones.

11. Lapham, "Tentacles of Rage," p. 38.

CHAPTER NINE

Town Hall Politics as Zombie Theater

Rethinking the Importance of the Public Sphere

The bitter debate that unfolded over Obama's health care plan garnered a great deal of media attention. The images were both familiar and disturbing—members of Congress being shouted down, taunted, hanged in effigy, and in some instances receiving death threats. In some cases, mob scenes produced violence and resulted in a number of arrests. Increasingly, people were showing up with guns at these meetings, revealing an intimate connection between an embrace of violence, politics, and a disturbing hatred of both the public sphere and the conditions for real exchange, debate, and dialogue over important social issues. Rowdy, zombie-like crowds, many of whom read from talking points made available to them by right-wing groups and legitimated by conservative television pundits, embraced a politics reminiscent of the Brown Shirts, whose task in Germany in the 1930s was to disrupt oppositional meetings, beat up opponents of the Nazi or Fascist Parties, and intimidate those individuals and groups that criticized authoritarian ideology.

This is not meant to suggest that all of the protestors at these meetings were members of extremist groups as much as it seeks to reveal the deep historical affinity such mob tactics have with dangerous authoritarian tendencies, many of which are irresponsibly sanctioned both by politicians such as Republican Senator Tom Coburn and right-wing television hosts such as Glenn Beck and Sean Hannity.[1] Of course, what started out as random meetings soon became a coordinated attempt to build an organized political machine, which has mushroomed into what has been called the Tea Party movement.[2] The United States is neither Nazi

Germany nor fascist Italy. What is important to recognize in light of these violent tendencies in the culture is Hannah Arendt's prescient warning that elements of totalitarianism continue to be with us and that rather than being relegated to the dustbin of history, the "still existing elements of totalitarianism would be more likely to crystallize into new forms."[3] These tendencies have been around for the last twenty years in the form of militarism, religious fundamentalism, a rabid Economic Darwinism, and a growing violence against the poor, immigrants, dissenters, and others marginalized because of their age, gender, race, ethnicity, and color.

What is new under the Obama regime is that the often hidden alliance between corporate power and the forces of extremism is now both celebrated and highly visible in the culture. What is novel is that the production of symbolic violence and the organized attempts to undermine the most basic principles of democracy are now embraced, if not showcased, as a register of patriotism and fueled by talk-radio extremists and the Rupert Murdoch media empire. For example, Fox News' Glenn Beck mixes his anti-government diatribes with the language of radical militia groups. Beck has warned President Obama that "The second American revolution is being played out right now . . . what is ahead may loosen the bonds of society," and it may end with "a French Revolution." Endlessly capitalizing upon fear and insecurity, Beck warns his audience that "[I]f we don't have some common sense, we're facing the destruction of our country . . . it's coming."[4] Eric Boehlert gets it right in claiming that what we are currently "witnessing is a militia rerun. Except this time, thanks to the likes of Beck and Fox News, the unwanted repeat is being broadcast nationwide."[5] Increasingly, politics is being emptied of any substance as citizens are reduced to obedient recipients of power by both the dominant media and by a number of politicians at the highest level of government. Shaming and silencing those who are at odds with right-wing and corporate views of the world have become a national pastime or, as the Fox News pundits would argue, just a matter of common sense.

Some have referred to these groups as mobs, but that distinction does not hold since many of the protesters are being fed talking points and are well organized to target very specific Democratic Congressional representatives and increasingly any currently elected politician. Mob rule is often spontaneous, while these rowdy, gun-toting, and increasingly violent groups are being organized and legitimated through the money and power of the insurance industry, lobbying groups such as FreedomWorks, anti-government politicians, racist fringe groups, and elements of the white militia. Many of them echo the type of anti-government extremism reminiscent of Timothy McVeigh, the Oklahoma bomber. As Frank Rich points out,

Anyone who was cognizant during the McVeigh firestorm would recognize the old warning signs re-emerging from the mists of history. The Patriot movement. "The New World Order," with its shadowy conspiracies hatched by the Council on Foreign Relations and the

Trilateral Commission. . . . White supremacists. Militias . . . [and what] the Southern Poverty Law Center had found in its report last year: the unhinged and sometimes armed anti-government right that was thought to have vaporized after its Oklahoma apotheosis is making a comeback. And now it is finding common cause with some elements of the diverse, far-flung and still inchoate Tea Party movement. All it takes is a few self-styled "patriots" to sow havoc.[6]

This is a movement of older white Americans who are generally uninformed politically, eager to eliminate most government agencies, and harbor an acute disdain for debate, thoughtfulness, and dialogue. There is a chilling similarity between their hatred of government and McVeigh's claim that "I reached the decision to go on the offensive—to put a check on government abuse of power."[7] In other words, they hate and even view as a pathology any vestige of democratic governance, politics, and representation. They are part of a fringe element within the GOP that has moved increasingly from the margins to the center of power.[8] They have already played a prominent role in electing Scott Brown from Massachusetts to the U.S. Senate, enabled Rand Paul, a card-carrying Tea Party founder, to win the Kentucky Republican senatorial primary, and successfully ran a number of candidates for public office.

While the media have often focussed, if not cashed in, on the rowdiness of Tea Party members, they have been represented largely as simply angry citizens with another point of view, as opposed to being members of a deeply authoritarian campaign to both disrupt Obama's reform agenda and to gut and destroy those spaces in American society where democracy can be nourished. Such attempts at balance undermine serious reporting and are politically disingenuous. Such groups have to be understood as being organized not merely for the production of symbolic and real violence, but also as a growing extremist movement that promotes a wilful misreading of the meaning of freedom, security, and human rights. What is crucial to recognize is that the groups who were shouting out and disrupting health care meetings are also the same people who want to privatize and corporatize public schooling, eliminate all traces of the social state, and destroy all remnants of those public spheres that promote critical literacy, civic courage, and non-commodified values that give meaning to a democracy.

These are the folks who encouraged members of the Florida legislature to pass a law that outlawed historical interpretation in Florida public schools.[9] These are the same groups for whom any vestige of education that promotes critical agency, self-representation, and promotes democracy is condemned—or worse, simply dispatched to the garbage can of educational practices. They are deeply xenophobic and appear to support fully Arizona's reactionary anti-immigrant bill. It is impossible to understand what these groups represent unless they are seen as part of an authoritarian tradition that has gained enormous strength in the last twenty years as part of a broader effort to corporatize civil society, militarize everyday life, criminalize the effects of social problems, privatize public goods, eviscerate any viable notion of the social, govern society through the laws of the marketplace, and destroy those public spaces where norms and democratic values are produced and constantly renewed.

Viewed primarily as either an economic investment or with unadulterated disdain, the public sphere is being undermined as a central democratic space for fostering the citizen-based processes of deliberation, debate, and dialogue. The important notion that space can be used to cultivate citizenship is now transformed by a new "common sense" that links it almost entirely to the production of consumers or to a pathologized space that bears the imprint of immigrants and those others now viewed with contempt by the nativism of right-wing groups and their televised spokespersons. The inevitable correlate to this logic is that providing space for democracy to grow is no longer a priority. As theorists such as Jürgen Habermas and David Harvey have argued, the idea of critical citizenship cannot flourish without the reality of public space.[10] Put differently, "the space of citizenship is as important as the idea of citizenship."[11]

As a political category, space is crucial to any critical understanding of how power circulates, how disciplinary practices are constructed, and how social control is organized. Public space as a political category performs invaluable theoretical work in connecting ideas to material struggles, theories to concrete practices, and political operations to the concerns of everyday life. Without public space, it becomes more difficult for individuals to imagine themselves as political agents or to understand the necessity for developing a discourse capable of defending civic institutions. Public space confirms the idea of individuals and groups having a public voice, thus drawing a distinction between civic liberty and market liberty.

The demands of citizenship affirm the social as a political concept in opposition to its conceptualization as a strictly economic category. The sanctity of the traditional town hall or public square in American life is grounded in the crucial recognition that citizenship has to be cultivated in non-commercialized spaces, informed by non-commercial civic values. Such spaces mark both the importance of the public and the need for spheres where dialogue, debate, and reason prevail against the production of civic illiteracy, violence, and mob rule. Indeed, democracy itself needs public spheres where critical education as a condition for democracy can be renewed, where people can meet, and democratic identities, values, and relations have the time "to grow and flourish."[12] The organized disruptions of town meetings, coupled with a growing Tea Party movement that appears to harbor more hate than insight, should not cancel out but renew the historical importance of public spaces. Such spaces are crucial for nourishing civic discourses and offering counter-movements to fight the current disappearance of democratic public spheres as significant spaces in which powerful states, corporations, groups, and individuals can be held directly accountable for the ethical and material effects of their decisions.

The hostile town meetings we witnessed in 2009 and 2010 are symptomatic of a growing authoritarianism in the United States, mobilized through an ongoing culture of fear and a form of patriotic correctness designed to bolster a rampant nationalism and a selective populism. One consequence of such a move is the demise of the promise of a vibrant democracy and the corresponding impoverishment of political life, increasingly manifested in the inability of a society to question itself, engage in critical dialogue, and translate private problems into social issues. This is a position that both characterizes and threatens any viable notion of democracy in the United States in the current historical moment. In a post–9/11 world, the space of shared responsibility has given way to the space of private fears and larger corporate interests. Politics is now mediated through a spectacle of mob rule in which fear and violence become the only modalities through which to grasp the meaning of the self and larger social relations. As the public collapses into highly charged narratives of personal anger, reason is uncoupled from freedom and the triumph of civic illiteracy, suggesting that irrational mob rule becomes "the only politics there is, the only politics with a tangible referent or emotional valence."[13]

Stripped of its ethical and political importance, the public has been largely reduced to a space where private interests are displayed, and the social order increasingly mimics a giant reality TV show where notions of the public register as simply a conglomeration of private woes, violent outbursts, and an unchecked hatred for dissent and dialogue. Most importantly, as everyday politics is decoupled from its democratic moorings, it becomes more difficult for people to develop a vocabulary for understanding how private problems and public issues constitute the very lifeblood of a vibrant politics and democracy itself. Emptied of any substantial content, democracy appears imperiled as individuals are unable to translate their privately suffered misery into public concerns and collective action.

As the social is devalued and public discourse and politics disappear, only to be replaced by unruly mobs emboldened by right-wing celebrities and politicians "to become part of the mob," "shout out," and "rattle" speakers, what emerges is not simply an ugly display of individuals and groups mobilized by lobbyist-run groups such as FreedomWorks and Americans for Prosperity. On the contrary, more than health care reform is under attack. What is truly under attack is any artifact of a democratic society that is at odds with a free-market fundamentalism and the dominant financial and economic interests that benefit from it.

Politics takes many forms, but central to it is the need for individuals, groups, and social movements to be able to translate individual problems into public concerns, to have informed opinions, and to create spaces where power is held accountable. The town hall fiascos are important, but they are only symptomatic of a larger assault against the social contract, the social state, public spheres, and democratic governance. And when read in this context, the challenge presented by these manufactured spectacles can be used to raise the level of the analysis and public conversation about the historical, economic, and political context which has nourished them and what must be done to address the larger threat and problems they pose to American democracy. Clearly, any response to such outbursts and threats posed by the growing Tea Party movement must be seen as part of a broader effort to address the importance of critical education, civic literacy, social responsibility, as well as the need to raise important questions about what education and civic literacy should accomplish in a democracy and what might such a politics capable of taking up this challenge look like.

NOTES

1. Frank Rich, "The Guns of August," *The New York Times* (August 23, 2009), p. WK8.
2. See David Barstow's extensive investigation of the Tea Party movement in his "Tea Party Lights Fuse for Rebellion on the Right," *The New York Times* (February 15, 2010), p. A1.
3. Elisabeth Young-Bruehl, *Why Arendt Matters* (New Haven: Yale University Press, 2006), p. 46. Of course, this issue is taken up by Hannah Arendt in her classic *Origins of Totalitarianism* (1951; rev. ed. New York: Schocken, 2004).
4. Cited in Eric Boehlert, "How Glenn Beck Helps Violent Right-Wing Militias," *AlterNet* (April 7, 2010), www.alternet.org/story 146341.
5. Ibid.
6. Frank Rich, "The Axis of the Obsessed and the Deranged," *The New York Times* (February 28, 2010), p. WK10.
7. Cited in Boehlert, "How Glenn Beck Helps Violent Right-Wing Militias."
8. See Adele M. Stan, "Inside Story on Town Hall Riots: Right-Wing Shock Troops Do Corporate America's Dirty Work," *AlterNet* (August 10, 2009), www.alternet.org/module/printversion/141860.
9. Robert Jensen, "Florida's Fear of History: New Law Undermines Critical Thinking," *Common Dreams.org* (July 17, 2006), http://www.commondreams.org/views06/0717–22.htm.
10. See Jürgen Habermas, *Jürgen Habermas on Society and Politics: A Reader* (Boston: Beacon Press, 1989) and David Harvey, *The New Imperialism*,(New York: Oxford University Press, 2003). The literature on the politics of space is far too extensive to cite, but of special interest are Michael Keith and Steve Pile, eds., *Place and the Politics of Identity* (New York: Routledge, 1993); Doreen Massey, *Space, Place, and Gender* (Minneapolis: University of Minnesota, 1994); and Margaret Kohn, *Radical Space: Building the House of the People* (Ithaca: Cornell University Press, 2003).
11. Jo Ellen Green Kaiser, "A Politics of Time and Space," *Tikkun* 18.6 (2003), pp. 17–19.
12. Kaiser, pp. 17–18.
13. Jean Comaroff and John L. Comaroff, "Millennial Capitalism: First Thoughts on a Second Coming," *Public Culture* 12:2 (2000), pp. 305–306.

CHAPTER TEN

Reclaiming Public Values in the Age of Casino Capitalism

This is a difficult time in American history. Economic meltdowns, massive unemployment, corporate-induced ecological disasters in the Gulf of Mexico, and a growing disdain for liberal and progressive politics that has gained enormous currency since the election of Barack Obama to the presidency. The American people have every right to demand to live in peace, enjoy the comforts of economic security, have access to decent health care, be able to send their children to quality schools, and live with a measure of security. Yet at a time when public values are subordinated to the rationality of profits, exchange values, and unbridled self-interest, politics becomes corrupt, devoid of critical agents, and reduced to empty rituals largely orchestrated by those who control the wealth, income, media, and commanding institutions of American society. As we have just witnessed in the debate on health care reform, the interests of the vast majority of American people in a public option and the extension of Medicare have been totally lost on a Congress that has been corrupted by power and its comfortable and shameful relations with those who control the military-industrial-academic complex. The Republican Party minority in the Senate did everything they could to prevent the further lengthening of a six-month extension of emergency jobless benefits for the millions of long-term unemployed Americans, many of whom are barely able to survive and have given up all hope. Such tactics once again proving that at the core of their policies is a desire to sap every element of life out of any viable notion of the social state.

Public values, public spheres, and the notion of the common good are viewed by too many politicians as either a hindrance to the goals of a market-driven society, or they are simply treated as a burden on the society, viewed as a sign of weakness, if not a pathology. Ethical considerations and social responsibility are now devalued, if not disdained, in a society wedded to short-term investments, easy profits, and a mode of economics in which social costs are increasingly borne by the poor while financial and political benefits are reaped by the rich. Unchecked self-interest and ruthless, if not trivial, modes of competition now replace politics or at least become the foundation for politics as complex issues are reduced to friend/enemy, winner/loser dichotomies. The crass Social Darwinism played out on reality TV now finds its counterpart in the politics of both the Democratic and Republican Parties. For instance, the Republican Party's only identifying ideology is that it is against anything that supports the common good and undercuts the profits of corporations and the rich. At the same time, Democrats have given up any vestige of a progressive politics and vision, aligning their ideals to conform to the interests of the lobbyists who now represent the not-so-invisible shadow government.[1]

Instead of public spheres that promote dialogue, debate, and arguments with supporting evidence, we have a national entertainment state with its multiple public and private spheres that infantilizes almost everything it touches, while offering opinions that utterly disregard evidence, truth, and civility.[2] Politics has come under the sway of multiple forms of fundamentalism, becoming more militarized, privatized, and divorced from any notion of the common good or public welfare. Violence saturates the culture, a brutalizing masculinity fuels the militarization of everyday life, and a collective ignorance is fueled by the assumption that intelligence and thoughtfulness should be dismissed as a form of elitism. Populism, or at least the Sarah Palin version, has little resemblance to genuine resistance to the anti-democratic tendencies in American society and now plays out as a homage to illiteracy and stupidity. Screen culture in its many manifestations signals if not celebrates the collapse of politics and the coming apocalypse. Making the world a better place has given way to collective narratives about how to survive alone in a world whose destruction is just a matter of time. Death, fear, and insecurity trump crucial questions about what it means to apprehend the conditions to live a good life in common with others. Not only is the issue of the good life and the conditions that make it possible often lost in the babble of the infotainment state, but the market values that produced the economic crisis have so devalued the concept and practice of democracy that Americans find it hard to even define its meaning outside of the sham of money-driven elections and the freedom to shop.

In the last decade, the representative functions of democracy have not only taken a steep dive in light of a political system whose policies are shaped by powerful corporations and the imperatives of the rich but also made largely dysfunctional because of a morally and politically bankrupt electoral system intimately tied to wealth and power. The dominant media largely function as a form of moral anesthesia and political firewall that legitimates a ruthless and failed free-market system while refusing to make visible the workings of a casino capitalism that rejects as a weakness any measure of compassion, care, trust, and vulnerability. As the values and interests of the market become a template for all of society, the only institutions, social relations, public spheres, and modes of agency that matter are those that pay homage to the rule of mobile capital and the interests of financial titans.

What the current financial crisis has revealed has less to do with the so-called greed of Wall Street moguls than with the increasing fragility of a market-driven system that produces inequalities in every sphere of life, making its ode to democracy and the good life a a dishonest fiction. Moreover, the formative culture that legitimates market fundamentalism and market democracy does more than erase any trace of self-regulation and public accountability; it also eliminates the language of self-reflection along with any form of productive discourse about the common good, public welfare, and the conditions that make all life worth living. Market-driven culture rejects the assumption that freedom is a shared experience in which self-interest is subordinated to the affirmation of public values, the common good, and the notion of social responsibility implied in recognizing and transforming the conditions that make the lives of others precarious. As Judith Butler masterfully puts it:

> Precariousness implies living socially, that is, the fact that one's life is always in some sense in the hands of the other. It implies exposure both to those we know and to those we do not know; a dependency on people we know, or barely know, or know not at all. Reciprocally, it implies being impinged upon by the exposure and dependency of others, most of whom remain anonymous. These are not necessarily relations of love or even of care, but constitute obligations toward others, most of whom we cannot name and do not know, and who may or may not bear traits of familiarity to an established sense of who "we" are. In the interest of speaking in common parlance, we could say that "we" have such obligations to "others" and presume that we know who "we" are in such an instance. The social implication of this view, however, is precisely that the "we" does not, and cannot, recognize itself, that it is riven from the start, interrupted by alterity, as Levinas has said, and the obligations "we" have are precisely those that disrupt any established notion of the "we."[3]

We have lived through a decade in which the call for security has lost any semblance of truth and political necessity and has become the legitimating code for imposing on the American people an imperial presidency—especially under George W. Bush and increasingly under Obama—undermined crucial civil liberties, and expanded the violence and terrorism associated with a permanent war economy and culture. Democracy thrives on dissent, but dissent and critical citizenship cannot take place in a country marked by a widening gap between political democracy and socio-economic power. Inequality is not just a normal outgrowth of a market-driven economy; it is fundamental to a political system that destroys democracy. A country that allows the power of multi-national corporations to be exempt from rule of democratic law and the responsible demands of a democracy has already lost the battle between balancing civil liberties and national security. Any call for further giving up of civil liberties suggests a dangerous silence about the degree to which civil liberties are already at risk and how the current call for national safety might work to further a different type of terrorism, one not marked by bombs and explosions, but by state-supported repression, the elimination of dissent, and the death of both the reality and promise of democracy.

At this time of national crisis, we need to recognize that the current economic recession cannot be understood apart from the crisis of democracy itself. It is all the more crucial, therefore, to recognize in a post–Gilded Age moment that those public spaces that traditionally have offered forums for debating norms, critically engaging ideas, making private issues public, and evaluating judgments are disappearing under the juggernaut of free-market values, corporate power, and intense lobbying pressure on the part of the country's most powerful financial institutions. Schools, universities, the media, and other aspects of the cultural education apparatus are being increasingly privatized or corporatized and removed from the discourse of the public good. Consequently, it becomes all the more crucial for educators, parents, social movements, and others to raise fundamental questions about what it means to revitalize a politics and ethics that takes seriously "such values as citizen participation, the public good, political obligation, social governance, and community."4

The call for a revitalized politics grounded in an effective democracy substantively challenges the dystopian practices of the new culture of fear and neoliberalism—with their all-consuming emphasis on insecurity, market relations, commercialization, privatization, and the creation of a world-wide economy of part-time workers—against their utopian promises. Such an intervention confronts Americans with the problem as well as challenge of developing those public spheres—such as the media, higher education, and other cultural institutions—that provide the conditions for creating citizens who are capable of exercising their freedoms, competent to question the basic assumptions that govern political life, and skilled enough to participate in developing broad social movements that will enable them to shape the basic social, political, and economic orders that govern their lives.

In spite of the fact that some notions of the public good have been recalled from exile in light of the economic recession and the election of Barack Obama, many young people and adults today still view the private as the only space in which to imagine any sense of hope, pleasure, or possibility. Not only is hope disappearing for this generation—which has been asked to give more but ask for less—but the economic and educational conditions that enable any sense of possibility for this generation are quickly disappearing. And while Obama and his priests of high finance have spent billions to bail out banks and conduct foreign wars, they have refused to implement an adequate jobs-creation program for young people and the millions of unemployed.

Market forces continue to focus on the related issues of consumption, excessive profits, and fear. Reduced to the act of consuming, citizenship is "mostly about forgetting, not learning,"[5] in spite of the hyped-up and increasing appeal to bearing the burden collectively of hard times—a burden that always falls on the shoulders of working people but not the banks or other commanding financial institutions. How else to explain the 2010 record profits of big banks and investment houses in the midst of an unflinching recession while millions lose their homes, jobs, and dignity? Moreover, as social visions of equity and justice recede from public memory, unfettered, brutal self-interests combine with retrograde social policies to make security and safety a top domestic priority. One consequence is that all levels of government are being hollowed out, reducing their role to dismantling the gains of the welfare state as they increasingly construct policies that now criminalize social problems, sell off public goods to the highest corporate bidders, and prioritize penal methods over social investments. Increasingly, notions of the public cease to resonate as a site of utopian possibility, as a fundamental space for how we reactivate our political sensibilities and conceive of ourselves as critical citizens, engaged public intellectuals, and social agents.

The growing lack of justice in American society rises in proportion to the lack of political imagination and collective hope.[6] We live at a time when the forces and advocates of a market-driven fundamentalism and militarism not only undermine all attempts to revive the culture of politics as an ethical response to the demise of democratic public life but also aggressively wage a war against the very possibility of creating non-commodified public spheres and forums that provide the conditions for critical education, link learning to social change, political agency to the defense of public goods, and intellectual courage to the refusal to surrender knowledge to the highest bidder. Understood as both a set of economic policies and an impoverished notion of citizenship, neoliberalism represents not just a series of market-driven programs but also a coherent set of cultural, political, and educational practices that mobilize communities around shared fears and collective insecurities.

Unlike some theorists who suggest that politics as a site of contestation, critical exchange, and engagement has either come to an end or is in a state of terminal arrest in light of the current calls for patriotic unity, I believe that the current depressing state of politics points to the urgent challenge of reformulating the crisis of democracy as part of a fundamental crisis of vision, meaning, education, and political agency. Politics devoid of a democratic vision either degenerates into cynicism or appropriates a view of power that appears to be equated only with domination. Lost from such accounts is the recognition that democracy has to be struggled over—even in the face of a most appalling crisis of political agency and threats to national security. There is also little attention paid to the fact that the struggle over politics and democracy is inextricably linked to creating public spheres where individuals can be educated as political agents equipped with the skills, capacities, and knowledge they need not only to actually perform as autonomous political agents but also to believe that such struggles are worth taking up. Central here is the assumption that politics is not simply about power but also, as the philosopher Cornelius Castoriadis points out, "has to do with political judgments and value choices,"[7] indicating that questions of civic education—learning how to become a skilled citizen—are central to both the struggle over political agency and democracy itself. Finally, there is the widespread refusal among many Americans and educators to recognize that the issue of civic education—with its emphasis on critical thinking, bridging the gap between learning and everyday life, understanding the connection between power and knowledge, and using the resources of history to extend democratic rights and identities—is not only the foundation for expanding and enabling political agency, but that such education takes place across a wide variety of public spheres through the very force of culture itself.

Any democratically inspired understanding of politics must challenge a casino politics that fills the social order and the sphere of politics with the walking dead. While the conditions for challenging casino politics may be under assault in what might be called a progressive administration, the basis for expanding and deepening democracy must be part of an ongoing struggle of engaged critique, civic courage, and organized collective struggles. Critical knowledge grounded in pressing social problems offers individuals and groups an important resource for shaping the conditions that bear down on their lives, enabling them to resist those forces that want to narrow the meaning of political freedom and social citizenship. The production of such knowledge must be connected to the urgent call to revitalize the language of civic education and ethical imagination as part of a broader discourse of political agency and critical citizenship in a global world.

Reclaiming the connection between the political and the ethical imagination as a pedagogical act may be one of the most crucial challenges facing the American public in the twenty-first century. If the institutions and conditions for a critical formative culture of questioning and civic engagement necessary for thinking beyond the narrow framing mechanisms of casino capitalism, militarism, and religious fundamentalism do not come into play, it is conceivable that the current economic recession will be repeated within a few short years, and American society will slip into a form of authoritarianism that will give up even its most dubious claims on democracy. The current crisis has systemic and ideological origins, and both must be addressed through a new political language in which ethical imagination couples with a sense of educated hope and the need for collective agents willing to build alternative public spheres and viable critical social movements.

We currently live in a society controlled by political and economic zombies. Under such circumstances, the coupling of cynicism and multiple forms of illiteracy undermines the possibility of critical thought, agency, and action. Public values or the public good, when they are invoked, are often couched in a nostalgic discourse about the New Deal or the Great Society. Rather than being viewed as a legacy that needs to be reclaimed, re-imagined, and renewed, visions of the public good and the public values they embody are sequestered to the historical past, put on display like a museum piece that is worth viewing but not an ideal worth struggling over. Corporate domination, power, abuse, and greed are once again being legitimated and argued for by a variety of right-wing movements in the United States, the most visible being the Tea Party movement. These movements do more than preach about God, money, and guns; they also sabotage democracy, block public debate about alternative forms of power, and try to sell the illusion, as Chris Hedges points out, "that the free market [is] a natural outgrowth of democracy and a force of nature" that we simply have to accept unquestionably.[8] Without an urgent reconsideration of the crucial place of public values in shaping American society, the meaning and gains of the past that extend from the Civil Rights movement to the antiwar movements of the 1960s will be lost, offering neither models nor examples of struggles forged in the heat of reclaiming democratic values, relations, and institutions.

New York Times columnist Frank Rich has argued that the most striking characteristic of the last decade is how much the American people have been conned, played for suckers with arguments about weapons of mass destruction, the genius of Karl Rove, and the importance of corporations in shaping our lives, to name a few of the lies.[9] Actually, as insightful as Rich is, he gets it backward. His claim that the American public has been fed a massive diet of illusions enabling a big con overlooks the power these ideas or deliberately shaped cons have as part of an official and legitimating ideology. These ideas are not illusions; they are the symbolic extensions of real and systemic power relations, and the often commonsense views they promote are powerful modes of legitimation. The issue that needs to be addressed is not simply about recognizing illusions but dismantling the socio-economic-educational forces that produce and circulate them as part of a larger framing of distinct and systemic power relations. If we are to reclaim any viable notion of the political along with the public values that give it meaning, we must address the primacy of pedagogy and critical inquiry as part of a broader attempt to revitalize the conditions for individual and social agency, while simultaneously addressing the most basic problems facing the prospects for social justice and global democracy. Public values matter, and they must become part of any ongoing attempt to give meaning to politics, the ethical imagination, and the promise of an aspiring democracy.

NOTES

1. See especially Thomas Frank, *The Wrecking Crew* (New York: Holt, 2009); David Cay Johnston, *Free Lunch: How the Wealthiest Americans Enrich Themselves at Government Expense* (New York: Portfolio, 2007).
2. On July 3, 2006, *The Nation* published an invaluable issue on The National Entertainment State.
3. Judith Butler, *Frames of War: When Is Life Grievable?* (Brooklyn, NY: Verso, 2009), pp. 13–14.
4. Carl Boggs, *The End of Politics* (New York: Guilford Press, 2000), p. ix.
5. Zygmunt Bauman, *Globalization: The Human Consequences* (New York: Columbia University Press, 1998), p. 82.
6. On this issue, see Roberto Mangabeira Unger and Cornel West, *The Future of American Progressivism* (Boston: Beacon Press, 1998).
7. Cornelius Castoriadis, "Institution and Autonomy," in Peter Osborne, *A Critical Sense: Interviews with Intellectuals* (New York: Routledge, 1996), p. 8.
8. Chris Hedges, *Empire of Illusion* (Toronto: Knopf Canada, 2009), p. 143.
9. Frank Rich, "Tiger Woods, Person of the Year," *The New York Times* (December 20, 2009), p. WK7.

SECTION III

Brutalizing Youth in the Age of Zombie Politics

CHAPTER ELEVEN

No Bailouts for Youth

Broken Promises and Dashed Hopes

By almost any political, economic, and ethical measure, Barack Obama's election victory in 2008 inherited a set of problems produced by one of the darkest periods in American history.[1] In the eight years prior to Obama's presidency, not only did the spaces where genuine politics could occur largely disappear as a result of an ongoing assault by the market-driven forces of privatization, deregulation, and unrestrained corporate power, but there was also a radical hardening of the culture that increasingly disparaged democratic values, the public good, and human dignity—and with these the safety nets provided by a once-robust but now exiled social state. George W. Bush, the privileged and profligate son of a wealthy Texas oilman, became the embodiment of a political era in which willful immaturity and stubborn civic illiteracy found its match in an emerging culture of excess and irresponsibility.[2] As the age of casino capital reigned supreme over American society, the ongoing work of democratization—along with the public spheres needed to sustain it—became an increasingly fragile, perhaps even dysfunctional, project. Market principles now reached far beyond the realm of the economic and played a formative role in influencing and organizing every domain of human activity and interaction, while simultaneously launching a frontal attack on notions of a common good, public purpose, non-commodified values, and democratic modes of governing.

Yet even in the aftermath of the October 2008 global financial crisis and the historic election of Barack Obama as the 44th President of the United States, the vocabulary and influence of corporate power and hapless governance can still be heard as the expansion of market fundamentalism continues, albeit more slowly, along the trajectory of privileging corporate interests over the needs of the public good, ignoring the rising demands of millions of people struggling for economic, racial, and political justice. Tragically, the Obama administration seems complicit with what has become an element of common sense for a large and noisy segment of the populace—that the market, rather than politics, gives people what they want. President Obama does not talk about a much-needed jobs-creation program to address the massive hardships and suffering many people are experiencing. Instead, he gets his cues from Wall Street and now focuses on taming the budget deficit.[3] Nor does he talk about the crippling poverty, collapsing urban infrastructures, or the general despair that now grips the country. This state of affairs suggests not only a perilous future for the social state and a government willing to intervene on behalf of its citizens but also a dangerous view of governance in which economic priorities dominate and suppress important social needs rather than being carefully adjusted toward the goal of fostering a more just, more democratic society.

It appears ever more unlikely that the Obama administration will undo the havoc wrought by the Bush administration (itself the culmination of a decades-long trend toward market deregulation) or reverse the effects of a rampant free-market fundamentalism now unleashed across the globe. As the financial crisis looms large in the lives of the majority of Americans, government funds are used to bail out Wall Street bankers rather than being used to address either the growing impoverishment of the many people who have lost homes, jobs, and hope of a better future or the structural conditions that created such problems. In this scenario, a privileged minority retains the freedom to purchase time, goods, services, and security, while the vast majority of people are relegated to a life without protections, benefits, and safety supports. For those populations considered expendable, redundant, and invisible by virtue of their race, class, and age, life becomes increasingly precarious.

As I have mentioned throughout this book, youth, in particular, are assaulted by market forces that commodify almost every aspect of their lives, though different groups of young people bear unequally the burden of this market-driven assault. Those who are marginalized by class and power suffer more than the indignity of being endlessly commodified and commercially carpet-bombed. They are also objects of a low-intensity war that now criminalizes their behavior, subjects increasing aspects of their lives to harsh disciplinary practices, and treats them as both dangerous and disposable. In a society in which the social state that has been hollowed out and largely stripped of its welfare functions, youth are no longer provided with the economic, social, and cultural supports that offer them dignity, prosperity, and the promise of a better future. Instead, they are now largely governed by a corporate state that "secures power through the imposition of law, discipline and uncompromising modes of punishment and imprisonment."[4]

As the mechanisms of power, containment, and policing merge, the spaces that young people inhabit become increasingly militarized. At the same time such hyper-militarized spaces, extending from the street to the school, are abetted by a cultural apparatus and public pedagogy that jump at every opportunity to demean and demonize young people, especially poor minority youth, by representing them as an ever-present threat to society. In this instance, it becomes all too easy for the American public to move from the notion of young people being troubled to viewing them as trouble, as a threat to be contained. Newspapers and other popular media treat their audiences to an endless stream of alarming images and dehumanizing stories about rampaging young people who allegedly occupy a domestic war zone. Youth are no longer categorized as Generation X, Y, or Z. On the contrary, they are now defined rhetorically in mainstream media as "Generation Kill," "Killer Children," or, as one CNN special labeled them, "Killers in Our Midst."[5] Capitalizing on shocking and sensational imagery not only swells the media's bottom line; it also adds fuel to a youth panic that insidiously portrays young people as pint-size nihilists and an ever-present threat to public order. Such negative and demeaning views have had disastrous consequences for young people as their lives are increasingly subjected to policies and modes of governance defined through the logic of punishment, surveillance, and penal control. Moreover, under the reign of an expanding punishing state, coupled with the persistent structural racism of the criminal justice system, the situation for a growing number of impoverished young people and youth of color is getting much worse.

These are young people whose labor is unneeded, who are locked out of the commodity market, and who often inhabit the impoverished and soul-crushing margins of society. Too often they fall prey to the dictates of a youth-crime-governing complex that increasingly subjects them to harsh disciplinary controls while criminalizing more and more aspects of their behavior. How else to explain that on any given day "one in every 10 young male high school dropouts is in jail or juvenile detention?"[6] What kind of sense does it make to pass truancy laws in which a student, even when he has a school pass that allows him to be out of classes early, is stopped by the police and issued a $570 ticket for truancy?[7] How can we reconcile the rise of zero tolerance laws in schools with the presumption that schools should be places where young people can feel safe and receive an education that prepares them to be thoughtful, critical, and socially responsible citizens when such laws impose harsh penalties for often trivial infractions, increase rates of suspension and expulsion, disproportionately target African American youth, push poor young people out of school and often into the criminal justice system? According to the Advancement Project,

Zero tolerance has engendered a number of problems: denial of education through increased suspension and expulsion rates, referrals to inadequate alternative schools, lower test scores, higher dropout rates, and racial profiling of students. . . . Once many of these youths are in "the system," they never get back on the academic track. Sometimes, schools refuse to readmit them; and even if these students do return to school, they are often labeled and targeted for close monitoring by school staff and police. Consequently, many become demoralized, drop out, and fall deeper and deeper into the juvenile or criminal justice systems. Those who do not drop out may find that their discipline and juvenile or criminal records haunt them when they apply to college or for a scholarship or government grant, or try to enlist in the military or find employment. In some places, a criminal record may prevent them or their families from residing in publicly subsidized housing. In this era of zero tolerance, the consequences of child or adolescent behaviors may long outlive students' teenage years.[8]

Where is the collective anger over the use of disciplinary policies that share a shameful and close affinity to the legacy of segregated education, slavery, racial targeting, the harsh and ruthless criminalization of poor white and minority youth, and pedagogies of punishment, all of which push young people out of school and into the criminal justice system? In this instance, schools neither educate nor provide even minimal training for the workplace. Instead, they simply mimic traditional lockdown institutions such as the prison and display a disdain for youth that offers no apologies because politicians, school boards, administrators, and some teachers have become too arrogant and ruthless to imagine any resistance. Wedded to the bloodless values of a market-driven society deeply implicated in reproducing the structures of racism, inequality, and exclusion, schools now inhabit a "dead zone" that banishes civic pedagogy, the arts, and different critical modes of intelligibility. Schools now do everything they can to deaden the imagination by defining and framing classroom experiences through a lethal mix of instrumental values, cost-benefit analyses, test-based accountability schemes, and high-stakes testing regimes. These instrumentally- and market-based values and practices drown out, if not repress, those spaces and pedagogical practices that provide the conditions for students to think critically, value their own voices, mobilize their curiosity, engage in shared learning, and—most of all—acquire the knowledge, habits, public values, and social relations necessary for the practice of empowerment necessary for fostering a real democracy and taking responsibility for sustaining it. More and more, it appears that as schools become more militarized and subject to the latest technologies of regulation, surveillance, and control, they are transformed into laboratories in which the limits of new authoritarian tendencies endemic to a corporate/punishing society are tamed, attenuated, and tested.[9]

Where is the moral outrage over a nation that incarcerates one in one hundred adults in its local, state, and federal prisons and jails, fragmenting families, desolating communities, and ruining the lives of millions of children?[10] Where are the intellectuals, parents, teachers, and social movements expressing political indignation over a country that has the onerous and dubious distinction of being the world's leading jailer of young people? Where is the moral wrath over the racist practices that lead to the increasing criminalization of African American youth, particularly those who drop out of schools with "nearly one in four young black male dropouts incarcerated or otherwise institutionalized on an average day."[11] As one politician noted, "Dropping out of high school [has become] an apprenticeship for prison."[12]

The devastation wreaked by free-market policies has been largely financed in the hard currency of human suffering that such policies have imposed on children, readily evident in some astounding statistics that suggest a profound moral and political contradiction at the heart of one of the richest democracies in the world. The notion that children should be treated as a crucial social resource and represent for any healthy society important ethical and political considerations about the quality of public life, the allocation of social provisions, and the role of the state as a guardian of public interests appears to be lost. Children, for example, make up a disproportionate share of the poor in the United States in that "they are 26 per cent of the total population, but constitute 39 per cent of the poor."[13] Just as alarmingly, prior to the passage of the health care reform bill, over 8 million children lacked health insurance,[14] and millions lacked affordable child care and decent early childhood education. One of the most damaging statistics revealing how low a priority children are in America can be seen in the fact that among the industrialized nations in the world, the United States ranks first in billionaires and in defense expenditures and yet ranks an appalling twenty-ninth in infant mortality.[15] As we might expect, behind these grave statistics lie a series of decisions to favor those already advantaged economically at the expense of the poor and socially vulnerable. Moreover, for the last three decades we have witnessed, especially under the second Bush administration, savage cuts to education, scientific research, and social services such as nutritional assistance for impoverished mothers and veterans' medical care—all of which helped fund tax breaks for the inordinately rich. Sadly, it now seems reasonable to assume that under the current financial crisis non-privileged youth will experience even greater economic and educational hardships, while becoming even more invisible to the larger society.

The toll in human suffering that results from these policies of punishment and neglect becomes clear in shocking stories about poor white and minority youth who literally die because they lack health insurance, often have to fend for themselves in the face of life's tragedies, and increasingly are excommunicated from the sphere of human concern. Too many youth are now rendered invisible and disposable in a world in which short-term investments yield quick profits while long-term social investments in young people are viewed as a drag on the economy. It gets worse. In what amounts to a national disgrace, one out every five children currently lives in poverty. Morever, while 10 percent of white children live in poverty, 34 percent of all black children live in poor families.[16] With home foreclosures still on the rise, school districts across the nation have identified and enrolled almost one million homeless children.[17] There are 1.7 million more children living in poverty today than in 2000. Unfortunately, their numbers are growing at an exponential rate, as 1 in 50 children and teens is now living in crowded rooms in seedy welfare hotels, in emergency shelters, or with relatives, or simply living on the streets.[18]

What is unique about these children and young people is not just the severity of deprivations they experience daily, but how they have been forced to view the world and redefine the nature of their own childhood between the borders of hopelessness and despair. There is little sense of a brighter future lying just beyond the shadows of highly policed and increasingly abandoned urban spaces. An entire generation of youth will not have access to the jobs, material comforts, or social securities available to previous generations. These children are a new generation of youth forced to grow up fast—they think, act, and talk like adults. They worry about their families, which may be headed by a single parent or both parents out of work and searching for a job; they wonder how their parents are going to get money to buy food and what it will take to pay for a doctor. And these children are no longer confined to so-called ghettoes. As the burgeoning landscape of poverty and despair spreads across our cities, suburbs, and rural areas, these children make their presence felt everywhere—there are just too many to ignore or hide away in the usually contained and invisible spaces of disposability. These young people constitute a new and more unsettling scene of suffering, one that reveals not only vast inequalities in our economic landscape but also portends a future that has no claim to a sprited notion hope, characteristic of an aspiring democracy.

We are treated endlessly to stories in which young people are robbed of their innocence as they are forced to worry about problems that are ordinarily the responsibility of adults. Too many children find themselves living in cars or seedy motels, or even worse, living on the streets. They think about getting jobs to help their parents buy food, put down money for an apartment, or simply get a motel room. Childhood concerns about dating, sports, and hanging out with friends are now replaced with more crucial, if not time-consuming and health-draining, concerns about surviving on a daily basis.

These narratives just scratch the surface of a new social and economic reality, as millions of children now find themselves suffering physical, psychological, and developmental problems that thus far have gone unacknowledged by the Obama administration, as it bails out the automotive industries, banks, and other financial institutions. What kind of country have we become that we cannot protect our children or offer them even the most basic requirements for survival? Where is the public indignation over an administration that provides a multi-billion-dollar gift to Wall Street but cannot develop a public works program to put poor white and minority youth to work? How can the American people put up with a government that is willing to subsidize and rescue the insurance giant American International Group but do virtually nothing to provide assistance for the nearly half of all U.S. children and 90 percent of black youth who will be on food stamps at some point in their childhood?

Everywhere we turn, we see untold amounts of hardship and human suffering among young and old alike. Millions of hard-working people have lost their jobs, homes, hopes, and in some cases their sanity, while Wall Street zombies flourish financially and reward their incompetence, failure, and moral indifference with lavish bonuses, punctuated with renewed efforts to prevent any of the reforms that would put a check on the corrupt practices that produced a global financial melt-down. What does it mean to witness this type of suffering among so many children and not do anything about it—our attentions quickly diverted to view the spectacles and moral indifference that characterize so much of the cut-throat world of reality TV, zombie politics, and a consumer culture that shapes the sensibilities and inner lives of adults and children alike? Obama's attraction to the cultural capital of the rich, his unwillingness to take risks, his Harvard-taught propensity for seeking middle ground, his increasing unwillingness to fight for the people who elected him, and his willingness to disconnect from his own pre-election ideals make him look increasingly not just weak but like a mere puppet of corporate power, an innocent who has been practically eaten alive by the rich and powerful who now treat him with a sense of scorn and derision only matched by their own moral vacuity and arrogance. Of course, this might suggest that I and others initially expected too much from Obama, but that is not the case. I realize that reforming the current problems facing the United States does not lie in the hands of one man but resides in changing the deeply structured economic and social relations of power and interests that inform a mode of casino capitalism that for all intents and purposes is out of control. At the same time, Obama must be held responsible for the decisions he has made—and, for the most part, those decisions that have shaped everything from financial regulation to educational reform are not on the side of working- and middle-class people but on the side of the rich and powerful.

At this moment in history, it is more necessary than ever to enter this debate over the fate of American democracy by registering youth as a central theoretical, moral, and political concern. Doing so reminds adults of their ethical and political responsibility to future generations and will further legitimate what it means to invest in youth as a symbol for nurturing civic imagination and collective resistance in response to the suffering of others. Young people provide a powerful referent for a critical discussion about the long-term consequences of casino capitalism and its hyper-market-driven policies, while also gesturing toward the need for putting into place those conditions that make a democratic future possible. We have been punishing children for a long time in the United States. Removed from the inventory of social concerns and the list of cherished public assets, young people have been either disparaged as a symbol of danger or simply rendered invisible.

Viewed as another casualty of the recession, youth are no longer included in a discourse about the promise of a better future. Instead they are now considered part of a disposable population whose presence threatens to recall repressed collective memories of adult responsibility in the service of a social contract and democratic ideals. Injustice and inequality have a long legacy in the United States, and their most punishing modes and lethal effects have been largely directed against poor white and minority children. The shameful condition of America's youth exposes not only their unbearable victimization but also those larger social and political forces that speak to the callous hardening of a society that actively produces the needless suffering and death of its children. The moral nihilism of a market society, the move from a welfare to a warfare state, the persistent racism of the alleged "raceless" society, the collapse of education into training, the deskilling of teachers and the militarizing of schools, the continued violations of civil liberties, the commodification of knowledge, and the rise of a pernicious corporate state work together to numb us to the suffering of others, especially children.

The crisis of youth is symptomatic of the crisis of democracy, and it calls us to account as much for the threat that it poses as for the challenges and possibilities it invokes. One way of addressing our collapsing intellectual and moral visions regarding young people is to imagine those policies, values, opportunities, and social relations that both invoke adult responsibility and reinforce the ethical imperative to provide young people, especially those marginalized by race and class, with the economic, social, and educational conditions that make life livable and the future sustainable. Clearly, the issue at stake here is not a one-off bailout or temporary fix but concrete structural economic, educational, and political reforms that provide everyone with real social, political, and individual rights and freedoms.

None of the problems facing this generation will be solved unless the institutions, social relations, and values that legitimate and reproduce current levels of inequality, power, and human suffering are dismantled, along with the formative culture that supports it. The very ideal of democracy has been hijacked by casino capitalism and its rampant structures of inequality and power. We catch a glimpse of what this means in Peter Dreier's observation that "Today, the richest one percent of Americans has 22 percent of all income and about 40 percent of all wealth. This is the biggest concentration of income and wealth since 1928."[19] This type of economic inequality is not merely incompatible with a functioning democracy, it makes democracy dysfunctional and corrupt. Just as government can no longer outsource its responsibilities, the American public can no longer allow its political system to be governed by the rich and powerful. Political culture has been emptied of its democratic values and is in free fall, as it is now largely shaped by the most powerful, politically corrupt, socially irresponsible, and morally tainted elements of the society. The widening gap between the rich and the poor has to be addressed if young people are to have a viable future. And that requires pervasive structural reforms that constitute a real shift in both power and politics away from a market-driven system that views too many children as disposable. We need to reimagine what liberty, equality, and freedom might mean as truly democratic values and practices.

Any society that endorses market principles as a template for shaping all aspects of social life and cares more about the accumulation of capital than it does about the fate of young people is in trouble. Next to the needs of the marketplace, life has become cheap, if not irrelevant. We have lived too long with governments and institutions that use power to promote violent acts, conveniently hiding their guilt behind a notion of state secrecy or lofty claims to democracy, while selectively punishing those considered expendable—in prisons, collapsing public schools, foster care institutions, and urban slums. Under the current regime of free-market casino capitalism, children lack power and agency and are increasingly viewed as either commodities or simply rendered disposable. If Barack Obama's call to address the crucial problems facing young people is to be taken seriously, then the political, economic, and institutional conditions that both legitimate and sustain a shameful attack on youth have to be made visible, open to challenge, and transformed. This can only happen by refusing the somnambulance and social amnesia that coincide with the pretense of a post-racial politics and the all-too-easy equation of free-market fundamentalism and democracy, especially given the effects such illusions have on those marginalized by class and color. The road to recovery must align itself with new social movements willing to take risks and that embrace a vision of a democracy that is on the side of children, particularly young children in need. It must enable the conditions for youth to learn—to "grow," as John Dewey once insisted, as engaged social actors more alive to their responsibilities to future generations than contemporary adult society has proven itself willing to be for them.

NOTES

1. I have taken up this issue in more detail in my *Against the Terror of Neoliberalism* (Boulder: Paradigm Publishers, 2008). See also Chris Hedges, *American Fascists: The Christian Right and*

the War on America (New York: Free Press, 2006); and Sheldon S. Wolin, *Democracy Incorporated: Managed Democracy and the Specter of Inverted Totalitarianism* (Princeton: Princeton University Press, 2008).

2. For an excellent analysis of this issue, see Chris Hedges, *Empire of Illusion: The End of Literacy and the Triumph of Spectacle* (New York: Knopf Canada, 2009). See also George Monbiot, "The Triumph of Ignorance," *AlterNet* (October 31, 2008), http://www.alternet.org/story/105447/the_triumph_of_ignorance:_how_morons_succeed_in_u.s._politics/. For an extensive study of anti-intellectualism in America, see Richard Hoftstadter, *Anti-Intellectualism in American Life* (New York: Vantage House, 1963); and Susan Jacoby, *The Age of American Unreason* (New York: Pantheon, 2008).

3. Paul Krugman, "The Phantom Menace," *The New York Times* (November 23, 2009), p. A27.

4. Judith Butler, *Frames of War: When Is Life Grievable?* (Brooklyn, NY: Verso, 2009), p. 5

5. "Generation Kill" is the name of a seven-part HBO miniseries about what *The New York Times* calls "a group of shamelessly and engagingly profane, coarse and irreverent marines . . . that spear-head[ed] the invasion" in the second Iraq war. See Alessandra Stanley, "Comrades in Chaos, Invading Iraq," *The New York Times* (July 11, 2008), p. B1. The term "Killer Children" appears as the title of a *New York Times* book review. See Kathryn Harrison, "Killer Children," *New York Times Book Review* (July 20, 2008), pp. 1, 8.

6. Andrew Sum et al., *The Consequences of Dropping Out of High School: Joblessness and Jailing for High School Dropouts and the High Cost for Taxpayers* (Boston: Center for Labor Market Studies, Northeastern University, October 2009), http://www.clms.neu.edu/publication/documents/The_Consequences_of_Dropping_Out_of_High_School.pdf.

7. Julianne Ong Hing, "Young, Brown—and Charged with Truancy," *Color Lines*, I52 (September/October 2009), www.colorlines.com/article.php?ID=593.

8. NAACP Legal Defense and Educational Fund, *Dismantling the School-to-Prison-Pipeline* (New York: Legal Defense Fund, 2009), http://www.jrclsconference.com/files/SpeakerMaterials/2009/Dismantling_the_School_to_Prison_Pipeline_BW_Version.pdf.

9. This idea comes from Zygmunt Bauman, *Society Under Siege* (Malden, MA: Blackwell Publishers, 2002), pp. 67–68.

10. See Pew Center for Research on the States, *One in 100* (Washington, DC, 2008).

11. Ibid.

12. Ibid.

13. . Cesar Chelala, "Rich Man, Poor Man: Hungry Children in America," *Seattle Times* (January 4, 2006), http://www.commondreams.org/views06/0104–24.htm.

14. The Henry J. Kaiser Family Foundation, *The Uninsured: A Primer* (October 2009), http://www.kff.org/uninsured/upload/7451–05.pdf.

15. Marian F. MacDorman and T.J. Mathews, *Recent Trends in Infant Mortality in the United States* (National Center for Health Statistics, October 2008), http://www.cdc.gov/nchs/data/databriefs/db09.htm.

16. Kenneth C. Land, *The 2009 Foundation for Child Development Child and Youth Well-Being Index (CWI) Report* (May 2009), http://www.fcd-us.org/usr_doc/Final-2009CWIReport.pdf. See also Sarah Fass and Nancy K. Cauthen, *Who Are America's Poor Children?: The Official Story*, National Center for Children in Poverty (October 2008), http://www.nccp.org/publications/pdf/text_843.pdf.

17. Kenneth C. Land, *Education for Homeless Children and Youths Program*, Foundation for Child Development (April 2009). Available online at: http://www.fcd-us.org/usr_doc/Final-

2009CWIReport.pdf.

18. National Center on Family Homelessness, *America's Youngest Outcasts: State Report Card on Child Homelessness* (March 2009), http://www.homelesschildrenamerica.org/pdf/rc_full_report.pdf.

19. Peter Dreier, "Bush's Class Warfare." See also Editors, "By the Numbers," *Inequality.Org* (October 14, 2007), http://www.demos.org/inequality/numbers.cfn.

CHAPTER TWELVE

Zero Tolerance Policies and the Death of Reason

Schools and the Pedagogy of Punishment

The shift to a society now governed through crime,[1] market-driven values, and the politics of disposability has radically transformed the public school as a site for a civic and critical education. One major effect can be seen in the increasingly popular practice of organizing schools through disciplinary practices that closely resemble the culture of the prisons.[2] For instance, many public schools, traditionally viewed as nurturing, youth-friendly spaces dedicated to protecting and educating children, have become one of the most punitive institutions many young people now face on a daily basis. Educating for citizenship, work, and the public good has been replaced with models of schooling in which students, especially poor minority youth, are viewed either as a threat or as perpetrators of violence. When not viewed as potential criminals, they are positioned as infantilized potential victims of crime (on the Internet, at school, and in other youth spheres) who must endure modes of governing that are demeaning and repressive. Jonathan Simon captures this transformation of schools from a public good to a security risk in the following comment:

> Today, in the United States, it is crime that dominates the symbolic passageway to school and citizenship. And behind this surface, the pathways of knowledge and power within the school are increasingly being shaped by crime as the model problem, and tools of criminal justice as the dominant technologies. Through the introduction of police, probation officers, prosecutors, and a host of private security professionals into the schools, new forms of

expertise now openly compete with pedagogic knowledge and authority for shaping routines and rituals of schools. . . . At its core, the implicit fallacy dominating many school policy debates today consists of a gross conflation of virtually all the vulnerabilities of children and youth into variations on the theme of crime. This may work to raise the salience of education on the public agenda, but at the cost to students of an education embedded with themes of "accountability," "zero tolerance," and "norm shaping."[3]

As the logic of the market and "the crime complex"[4] frame a number of social actions in schools, students are subjected to three particularly offensive policies, often defended by school authorities and politicians under the rubric of school safety. First, students are increasingly subjected to zero tolerance laws that are used primarily to punish, repress, and exclude them. Second, they are increasingly subjected to a "crime complex" in which security staff using harsh disciplinary practices now displace the normative functions teachers once provided both in and outside of the classroom. Third, more and more schools are breaking down the space between education and juvenile delinquency, substituting penal pedagogies for critical learning and replacing a school culture that fosters a discourse of possibility with a culture of fear and social control. Consequently, many youth, especially poor minorities in urban school systems, are not just being suspended or expelled from school but also have to bear the terrible burden of being ushered into the dark precincts of juvenile detention centers, adult courts, and prisons.

Once seen as an invaluable public good and laboratory for critical learning and engaged citizenship, public schools are increasingly viewed as a site of crime, warehouses, or containment centers. Consequently, students are also reconceived through the optic of crime as populations to be managed and controlled primarily by security forces. In accordance with this perception of students as potential criminals and the school as a site of disorder and delinquency, schools across the country since the 1980s have implemented zero tolerance policies that involve the automatic imposition of severe penalties for first offenses of a wide range of undesirable, but often harmless, behaviors. Based on the assumption that schools are rife with crime and fueled by the emergence of a number of state and federal laws such as the Gun-Free Schools Act of 1994, mandatory sentencing legislation, and the popular "three strikes and you're out" policy, many educators first invoked zero tolerance rules against kids who brought firearms to schools. This was exacerbated by the high-profile school shootings in the mid-1990s, the tragic shootings at Columbine High School on April 20, 1999, and the more recent shootings at Virginia Tech.

But as the climate of fear increased, the assumption that schools were dealing with a new breed of student—violent, amoral, and apathetic—began to take hold in the public imagination. Moreover, as school safety became a top educational priority, zero tolerance policies were broadened and now include a range of behavioral infractions that encompass everything from possessing drugs or weapons to threatening other students—all broadly conceived. Under zero tolerance policies, forms of punishment that were once applied to adults now apply to first graders. Students who violate what appear to be the most minor rules—such as a dress code violation—are increasingly subjected to zero tolerance laws that have a disparate impact on students of color while being needlessly punitive. The punitive nature of the zero tolerance approach is on display in a number of cases where students have had to face harsh penalties that defy human compassion and reason. An example is the recent high-profile case of Zachary Christie, a 6-year-old first grader, who received a 45-day suspension because he brought to school his favorite Cub Scout camping utensil, which can serve as a knife, fork, and spoon. Rather than being treated as a young boy who simply made a mistake, he was treated by the school as a suspect who deserved to be punished. It seems that the only thing being punished in this case was informed reason and critical judgment. Because of the national publicity the case received, school officials modified their decision and allowed the boy to return to school.

Most children who confront these harsh disciplinary procedures are not so lucky. One typical example is the case of an 8-year-old boy in the first grade at a Miami elementary school who took a table knife to his school, using it to rob a classmate of $1 in lunch money. School officials claimed he was facing "possible expulsion and charges of armed robbery."[5] In another incident that took place in December 2004, "Porsche, a fourth-grade student at a Philadelphia, PA, elementary school, was yanked out of class, handcuffed, taken to the police station and held for eight hours for bringing a pair of 8-inch scissors to school. She had been using the scissors to work on a school project at home. School district officials acknowledged that the young girl was not using the scissors as a weapon or threatening anyone with them, but scissors qualified as a potential weapon under state law."[6] It gets worse. Adopting a rigidly authoritarian zero tolerance school discipline policy, the following incident in the Chicago public school system signals both bad faith and terrible judgment on the part of educators implementing these practices. According to the report *Education on Lockdown*,

> In February 2003, a 7-year-old boy was cuffed, shackled, and forced to lie face down for more than an hour while being restrained by a security officer at Parker Community Academy on the Southwest Side. Neither the principal nor the assistant principal came to the aid of the first grader, who was so traumatized by the event he was not able to return to school.[7]

Traditionally, students who violated school rules and the rights of others were sent to the principal's office, guidance counselor, or another teacher. Corrective discipline in most cases was a matter of judgment and deliberation generally handled within the school by the appropriate administrator or teacher. Under such circumstances, young people could defend themselves, the context of their rule violation was explored (including underlying issues, such as problems at home, that may have triggered the behavior in the first place), and the discipline they received was suited to the nature of the offense. In other words, teachers and school administrators did what they were supposed to do: listen, exercise judgment and discrimination, and then decide how to handle an infraction. Today, in the age of standardized testing, thinking, and acting, reason and judgment have been thrown out the window just as teachers are increasingly being deskilled and forced to act as semi-robotic technicians good for little more than teaching for the test and serving as a reminder that we are arriving at a day when the school curriculum will be teacher-proof. Under the Obama administration, teacher unions are under attack, charter schools are viewed as the vanguard of reform, and teachers are forced into the role of clerks and technicians who are obliged to prepare students to take standardized tests.

The script is an old one, but it is even more damaging today as pedagogy is stripped not only of dissenting thought but of thought itself. What does it mean when Florida passes legislation claiming that only facts rather than interpretation can be taught in social studies classrooms? What does it say about the value of public education when Arizona bans ethnic studies on the grounds that it is divisive? Why isn't there public outrage over right-wing conservatives in Texas falsifying information presented in school textbooks in order to assert their own ideological ignorance—an ignorance that will now be taught to millions of students? The fog of stupidity and abuse now engulfs both teachers and students. And the result will be a generation of students deprived of the right to think critically, question authority, and develop a sense of autonomous agency.

This loss of autonomy produced by the sabotaging of critical education and the rise of a culture of security now defines schools through the narrow optics of measurement and discipline. Today, as school districts link up with law enforcement agencies, young people find themselves not only being expelled or suspended in record rates but also "subject to citations or arrests and referrals to juvenile or criminal courts."[8] Students who break even minor rules, such as pouring a glass of milk on another student or engaging in a schoolyard fight, have been removed from the normal school population, handed over to armed police, arrested, handcuffed, shoved into patrol cars, taken to jail, fingerprinted, and subjected to the harsh dictates of the juvenile and criminal justice systems.

How educators think about children through a vocabulary that has shifted from hope to punishment is evident in the effects of zero tolerance policies, which criminalize student behavior in ways that take an incalculable toll on their lives and their future. As the former nationally syndicated journalist Ellen Goodman pointed out, zero tolerance has become a code word for a "quick and dirty way of kicking kids out" of school.[9] This becomes clear as cities such as Denver and Chicago, in their eagerness to appropriate and enforce zero tolerance policies in their districts, do less to create a safe environment for students than simply kick more young people out of the public school system, and these are not the young people who attract the dominant media but poor white, brown, and black kids who increasingly are seen as disposable. For example, between 2000 and 2004, the Denver Public School System experienced a 71 percent increase in the number of student referrals to law enforcement, many for non-violent behaviors. The Chicago School System in 2003 had over 8,000 students arrested, often for trivial infractions such as pushing, tardiness, and using spitballs. As part of a human waste management system, zero tolerance policies have been responsible for suspending and expelling black students in record numbers. For instance, "in 2000, Blacks were 17 percent of public school enrollment nationwide and 34 percent of suspensions." And when poor black youth are not being suspended under the merger of school security and law-and-order policies, they are increasingly at risk of falling into the school-to-prison pipeline. As the Advancement Project points out, the racial disparities in school suspensions, expulsions, and arrests feed and mirror similar disparities in the juvenile and criminal justice systems.

> [I]n 2002, Black youths made up 16% of the juvenile population but were 43% of juvenile arrests, while White youths were 78% of the juvenile population but 55% of juvenile arrests. Further, in 1999, minority youths accounted for 34% of the U.S. juvenile population but 62% of the youths in juvenile facilities. Because higher rates of suspensions and expulsions are likely to lead to higher rates of juvenile incarceration, it is not surprising that Black and Latino youths are disproportionately represented among young people held in juvenile prisons.[10]

The city of Chicago, which has a large black student population, implemented a take-no-prisoners approach in its use of zero tolerance policies, and the racially skewed consequences are visible in grim statistics that reveal that "every day, on average, more than 266 suspensions are doled out . . . during the school year." Moreover, the number of expulsions has "mushroomed from 32 in 1995 to 3,000 in the school year 2003–2004,"[11] most affecting poor black youth.

As the culture of fear, crime, and repression dominates American public schools, the culture of schooling is reconfigured through the allocation of resources used primarily to hire more police, security staff, and technologies of control and surveillance. In some cases, schools such as the Palm Beach County system have established their own police departments. Saturating schools with police and security personnel has created a host of problems for schools, teachers, and students—not to mention that such policies tap into financial resources otherwise used for actually enhancing learning. In many cases, the police and security guards assigned to schools are not properly trained to deal with students and often use their authority in ways that extend far beyond what is either reasonable or even legal. When Mayor Giuliani in 1998 allowed control of safety to be transferred to the New York

City Police Department, the effect was not only a jump in the number of police and school safety agents but also an intensification of abuse, harassment, and arrests of students throughout the school system.

One example of the war-on-terror tactics used domestically and impacting schools can be seen in the use of the roving metal detector program in which the police arrive at a school unannounced and submit all students to metal detector scans. In *Criminalizing the Classroom*, Elora Mukherjee describes some of the disruptions caused by the program:

> As soon as it was implemented, the program began to cause chaos and lost instructional time at targeted schools, each morning transforming an ordinary city school into a massive police encampment with dozens of police vehicles, as many as sixty SSAs [School Security Agents] and NYPD officers, and long lines of students waiting to pass through the detectors to get to class.[12]

As she indicates, the program does more than delay classes and instructional time: it also fosters abuse and violence. The following incident at Wadleigh Secondary School on November 17, 2006, provides an example of how students are abused by some of the police and security guards. Mukherjee writes:

> The officers did not limit their search to weapons and other illegal items. They confiscated cell phones, iPods, food, school supplies, and other personal items. Even students with very good reasons to carry a cell phone were given no exemption. A young girl with a pacemaker told an officer that she needed her cell phone in case of a medical emergency, but the phone was seized nonetheless. When a student wandered out of line, officers screamed, "Get the fuck back in line!" When a school counselor asked the officers to refrain from cursing, one officer retorted, "I can do and say whatever I want," and continued, with her colleagues, to curse.[13]

Many students in New York City have claimed that the police are often disrespectful and verbally abusive, stating that "police curse at them, scream at them, treat them like criminals, and are on 'power trips.' . . . At Martin Luther King Jr. High School, one student reported, SSAs refer to students as 'baby Rikers,' implying that they are convicts-in-waiting. At Louis D. Brandeis High School, SSAs degrade students with comments like, 'That girl has no ass.'"[14] In some cases, students with severe health problems had their phones taken away and, when they protested, were either arrested or assaulted. Mukherjee reports that "A school aide at Paul Robeson High School witnessed a Sergeant yell at, push, and then physically assault a child who would not turn over his cell phone. The Sergeant hit the child in the jaw, wrestled him to the ground, handcuffed him, removed him from school premises, and confined him at the local precinct."[15] There have also been cases of teachers and administrators being verbally abused, assaulted, and arrested while trying to protect students from overzealous security personnel or police officers.

Under such circumstances, schools begin to take on the obscene and violent contours one associates with maximum security prisons: unannounced locker searches, armed police patrolling the corridors, mandatory drug testing, and the ever-present phalanx of lock-down security devices such as metal detectors, X-ray machines, surveillance cameras, and other technologies of fear and control. Appreciated less for their capacity to be educated than for the threat they pose to adults, students are now treated as if they were inmates, often humiliated, detained, searched, and in some cases arrested. Randall Beger is right in suggesting that the new "security culture in public schools [has] turned them into 'learning prisons' where the students unwittingly become 'guinea pigs' to test the latest security devices."[16]

Poor black and Latino male youth are particularly at risk in this mix of demonic representation and punitive modes of control as they are the primary object of not only racist stereotypes but also a range of disciplinary policies that criminalize their behavior.[17] Such youth, increasingly viewed as a burden and dispensable, now bear the brunt of these assaults by being expelled from schools, tried in the criminal justice system as adults, and arrested and jailed at rates that far exceed those of their white counterparts.[18] While black children make up only 15 percent of the juvenile population in the United States, they account for 46 percent of those put behind bars and 52 percent of those whose cases end up in adult criminal courts. Shockingly, in the land of the free and the home of the brave, "[a] jail or detention cell after a child or youth gets into trouble is the only universally guaranteed child policy in America."[19]

Students being miseducated, criminalized, and arrested through a form of penal pedagogy in lock-down schools that resemble prisons is a cruel reminder of the degree to which mainstream politicians and the American public have turned their backs on young people in general and poor minority youth in particular. As schools are reconfigured around the model of the prison, crime becomes the central metaphor used to define the nature of schooling, while criminalizing the behavior of young people becomes the most valued strategy in mediating the relationship between educators and students. The consequences of these policies for young people suggest not only an egregious abdication of responsibility—as well as reason, judgment, and restraint—on the part of administrators, teachers, and parents, but also a new role for schools as they become more prison-like, eagerly adapting to their role as an adjunct of the punishing state.

As schools define themselves through the lens of crime and merge with the dictates of the penal system, they eliminate a critical and nurturing space in which to educate and protect children in accordance with the ideals of a democratic society. As central institutions in the youth disposability industry, public schools now serve to discipline and warehouse youth, while they also put in place a circuit of policies and practices to make it easier for minority youth to move from schools into the juvenile justice system and eventually into prison. The combination of school punishments and criminal penalties has proven a lethal mix for many poor minority youth and has transformed schools from spaces of youth advocacy, protection, hope, and equity to military fortresses, increasingly well positioned to mete out injustice and humiliation, transforming the once-nurturing landscapes that young people are compelled to inhabit. Rather than confront the war on youth, especially the increasing criminalization of their behavior, schools now adopt policies that both participate in and legitimate the increasing absorption of young people into the juvenile and adult criminal justice system. Although state repression aimed at children is not new, what is unique about the current historical moment is that the forces of domestic militarization are expanding, making it easier to put young people in jail rather than provide them with the education, services, and care they need to face the growing problems characteristic of a democracy under siege. War abroad takes a toll not only in the needless loss of lives but also diverts valuable resources from expanding public goods, especially schools and the quality of life of the young people who inhabit them. As minority youth increasingly become the object of severe disciplinary practices in public schools, many often find themselves vulnerable and powerless as they are thrown into juvenile and adult courts or, even worse, into overcrowded and dangerous juvenile correctional institutions and sometimes adult prisons.

In this insufferable climate of increased repression and unabated exploitation, young people and communities of color become the new casualties in an ongoing war against justice, freedom, social citizenship, and democracy. Given the switch in public policy from social investment to a policy of testing, measurement, and punishment that President Obama and Secretary of Education Arne Duncan seem willing to support, it is clear that schools will continue to be the object of malign neglect, viewed less as a public good than a public pathology. Moreover, as government policy continues to push for high-stakes testing, militarizing schools, and addressing educational reform through the support of charter schools, it is clear that young people for whom race and class loom large have become disposable and will be the first to be neglected and eventually punished. After all, these are the young people who are viewed as needing more resources and services while in the end lowering test scores. According to the fact that schools today are viewed as instruments of production and adjuncts of the corporation, they are judged largely through that which can only be quantified. Consequently, public schools and the values and principles through which they organized have more in common with factories and prisons than with an education that prepares people to be knowledgeable, compassionate, and critically engaged citizens.

How much longer can a nation ignore those youth who lack the resources and opportunities that were available, in a partial and incomplete way, to previous generations? And what does it mean when a nation becomes frozen ethically and imaginatively in providing its youth with a future of hope and opportunity? Under such circumstances, it is time for parents, young people, educators, writers, labor unions, and social movements to take a stand and to remind themselves that not only do young people deserve more, but so does an aspiring democracy that has any sense of justice, vision, and hope for the future.[20]

NOTES

1. This concept comes from Jonathan Simon, *Governing Through Crime: How the War on Crime Transformed American Democracy and Created a Culture of Fear* (New York: Oxford University Press, 2007).
2. For an excellent analysis of this issue, see Christopher Robbins, *Expelling Hope* (Albany: SUNY Press, 2008); Valerie Polakow, *Who Cares for Our Children?* (New York: Teachers College Press, 2007); William Lyons and Julie Drew, *Punishing Schools: Fear and Citizenship in American Public Education* (Ann Arbor: University of Michigan Press, 2006); Henry A. Giroux, *The Abandoned Generation* (New York: Palgrave Press, 2004).
3. Simon, *Governing Through Crime*, p. 209.
4. This term comes from David Garland, *The Culture of Control: Crime and Social Order in Contemporary Society* (Chicago: University of Chicago Press, 2002).
5. Yolanne Almanzar, "First Grader in $1 Robbery May Face Expulsion," *The New York Times* (December 4, 2008), p. A26.
6. Advancement Project in partnership with Padres and Jovenes Unidos, Southwest Youth Collaborative, *Education on Lockdown: The Schoolhouse to Jailhouse Track* (Chicago: Children & Family Justice Center of Northwestern University School of Law, March 24, 2005), p. 11.
7. Ibid., p. 33.
8. Ibid., p. 7.
9. Ellen Goodman, "'Zero Tolerance' Means Zero Chance for Troubled Kids," *Centre Daily Times* (January 4, 2000), p. 8.
10. Advancement Project, *Education on Lockdown*, pp. 17–18.
11. Ibid., p. 31.
12. Elora Mukherjee, *Criminalizing the Classroom: The Over-Policing of New York City Schools* (New York: American Civil Liberties Union and New York Civil Liberties, March 2008), p. 9.
13. Ibid., p. 6.
14. Ibid., p. 16.
15. Ibid., p. 16.
16. Randall R. Beger, "Expansion of Police Power in Public Schools and the Vanishing Rights of Students," *Social Justice* 29:1 (2002), p. 120.
17. Victor M. Rios, "The Hypercriminalization of Black and Latino Male Youth in the Era of Mass Incarceration," in *Racializing Justice, Disenfranchising Lives*, ed. Marable, Steinberg, and Middlemass, pp. 40–54.
18. For a superb analysis of urban marginality of youth in the United States and France, see Loic Wacquant, *Urban Outcasts* (London: Polity, 2008).

19. Children's Defense Fund, *America's Cradle to Prison Pipeline* (Washington, DC: Children's Defense Fund, 2007), http://www.childrensdefense.org/child-research-data-publications/data/cradle-prison-pipeline-report-2007-full-highres.html., p. 77.
20. There are a growing number of groups fighting the growing school-to-prison pipeline, including the crucial work being done by the Children's Defense Fund under the leadership of Marian Wright Edelman and labor organizers such as Manuel Criollo, who works with the Labor/Community Strategy Center in Los Angeles, California, to end the destruction of the social welfare state and rise of a prison, punishment, and incarceration state. Under an initiative called the Community Rights Campaign, they are working with groups in California and in other states to end the school-to-prison pipeline and promote the broad work of educational justice. Their current campaign theme is "Not down with the Lock Down," and their demands include:

- Decriminalize Truancy—End Truancy Tickets for Tardiness or as a Discipline Measure (truancy in LA and around the country is the heightened 'broken window' policy—to curb daytime "crime" by busting tardiness and truancy)
- End School Administration Collaboration with the Gang Database—End Racist Profiling in Schools
- End Zero Tolerance & Police Repression in Our Schools & Communities
- Youth Mentors and Support Programs, not Probation
- Peer Conflict Mediation, not "Police Coercive Manipulation"
- Fully Fund Programs that Culturally Support Services for Students of Color

CHAPTER THIRTEEN

Brutalizing Kids

Painful Lessons in the Pedagogy of School Violence

Zombie politics has as one of its distinctive features the violence it wages against young people. For instance, on May 20, 2009, Marshawn Pitts, a 15-year-old African American boy who is also a special needs student, was walking down the corridor of the Academy for Learning High School in Dolton, Illinois. A police officer in the school noticed that the boy's shirt was not tucked in and started shouting and swearing at him. Pitts claims that he immediately started to tuck in his shirt, but it was too late. Within seconds, the police officer pushed him into the lockers, repeatedly punched him, and then slammed him to the ground and pushed his face to the floor. The officer then applied a face-down take-down hold to the child, a maneuver that has resulted in over twenty deaths nationwide and is banned in eight states. Pitts said he was terrified and was having a hard time breathing as a result of the forceful restraint. Because of this unprovoked attack by a police officer who is supposed to protect kids in school, the young man ended up with a broken nose and a bruised jaw.

In case the reader suspects I have confused the facts, the assault was caught on school security cameras and ended up on YouTube.[1] Indeed, a 15-year-old boy with an early childhood brain injury and a learning disorder, attending a school for special needs children, was tackled in the school and suffered injuries by a police officer because of a dress code violation. Pitts was not carrying a weapon. He did not threaten anyone. He was not dealing drugs. In fact, he appears to have given an entirely new meaning to what constitutes a clear and present danger, warranting the use of force by the police—he simply did not have his shirt tucked in, and for this he was beaten by a police officer three times his size. Harmless acts of indiscretion are now elevated to the status of a dangerous crime.

One could argue that this case is so bizarre and outrageous that the only logical explanation is to call into question the cop's (not the young man's) mental capacities. How could a reasonable adult trained as a professional policeman so viciously assault a young boy for no apparent or legitimate reason? But that is too easy. The brutalizing behavior exhibited by this unhinged police officer would be better understood as symptomatic of a set of larger forces in American society that are increasingly defining kids through a youth crime complex that touches almost every aspect of their lives—extending from the streets they walk on to the schools and community centers in which they spend most of their time.

This is not meant to suggest that school violence is not a real problem. Schools have an obligation to create safe environments for all of our children, environments that are welcoming rather than threatening, conducive to real learning, and attentive to the problems students face. Administrators and teachers should connect to student histories, be respectful of their experiences, encourage their voices, and protect their rights. At the same time, school safety must take seriously the broader educational goal of educating students "to participate in the complex and infinitely worthwhile labor of forming citizens, men and women capable of furthering what's best about us and forestalling what's worst."[2]

The tragic death of 16-year-old Chicago student Derrion Albert, captured on video and widely shown on the news;[3] the 49 school-age children who have been killed in Chicago by October 2009; the 300 wounded in 2009; and the fact that one recent study states that 61 percent of all school children are exposed to varying degrees of violence, speak to the culture of violence that young people face every day both in and out of schools. What bears repeating is that these acts of violence took place in and out of schools. School violence cannot be disconnected from the larger violence that filters through American society, nor can it be addressed by demonizing or beating kids, or, incredulously, militarizing their schools. Nor can it be understood by simply pumping money into cash-strapped schools to promote standardized testing, which borders on a kind of symbolic violence. The underlying economic, social, and political causes of violence are largely tied to a society in which young people, especially poor minority youth, simply do not matter any longer and are considered disposable. Removed from the discourse of social investment, if not the social contract itself, they are destined to be unemployed, having been warehoused in schools often lacking the most basic resources, and subject to a culture of violence from which they can rarely escape and almost never transform on their own.

In a society ruled by the living undead, young people are increasingly the victims of adult abuse and are maligned as dangerous and undeserving of even mild forms of social investment. Hence, it is not surprising, given how little money or time is spent on them, that they are treated as a threat, and their behavior endlessly monitored, controlled, and subject to harsh disciplinary measures. Schools, especially for poor white and minority children, are largely viewed as either testing centers where young people are simply bored into passivity or submission, or they are modeled after prisons—subject to punishing, zero tolerance policies, lockdowns, constant surveillance, humiliating security measures, intimidation, and sometimes assault, by security and police who are often armed and roam the corridors. In short, if you are poor black, brown, or white youth, you are not considered a viable student or a productive citizen but a potential criminal.

Schools now form partnerships with the police and private security agencies. Teachers, once the heroes in this coming-of-age narrative, are now a sideshow. Most are deskilled, reduced to technicians teaching for the high-stakes testing machine and often forced to share their responsibilities with armed security forces. Administrators now confuse management with leadership and become the pawns of corporate and punishing forces they can no longer control. Instead of investing in disadvantaged youth, American society now punishes them, and instead of being prepared for a productive life in the larger society, too many young people are pushed and shoved into a criminal justice system. They move from the schools directly to the juvenile detention centers, if not adult prisons. And when money is pumped into the schools, it is increasingly diverted from addressing real problems such as the need for more teachers, social workers, health workers, teaching aides, and safe avenues of protection for kids travelling to and from school. Instead, the money is invested in metal detectors, surveillance cameras, security guards, high security fences, and armed police with dogs.

While all youth are now suspect, poor minority youth have become the primary targets of modes of social regulation, crime control, and disposability—now the major prisms that define many of the public institutions and spheres that govern their lives. The model of policing that governs all kinds of social behaviors and interactions also constructs a narrow range of meaning through which young people define themselves. This rhetoric and practice of policing, surveillance, and punishment have little to do with the project of youth as the social investment of the future and a great deal to do with increasing powerful modes of disciplinary regulation, pacification, and control—elements comprising a "youth control complex" whose prominence in American society points to a state of affairs in which the claims of democracy go unheard.

Students being miseducated, mistreated, criminalized, and arrested through a form of penal pedagogy in locked-down schools that resemble prisons is a vicious and incredibly visible index of the degree to which mainstream politicians and the

American public have turned their backs on young people in general and poor minority youth in particular. As schools are reconfigured to resemble prisons, crime becomes the central metaphor used to define the school environment, while criminalizing the behavior of young people becomes the most valued strategy in mediating the relationship between educators and students. The consequences of these policies for young people suggest not only an egregious abdication of responsibility—as well as reason, judgment, and restraint—on the part of administrators, teachers, and parents, but also a new role for schools as they become more prison-like and more segregated as a consequence, eagerly adapting to their role as an adjunct of the punishing state.

One wonders how many more young people have to be brutalized in their schools and killed outside of schools before the American public wakes up and takes seriously not only its responsibility to young people but also its commitment to a mode of politics and a future that is on the side of young people rather than a vision shaped largely by the values of the corporate state and the disciplinary apparatuses of the punishing criminal justice system. What do the video of Marshawn Pitts being brutalized by a police officer and the equally heartbreaking video of Derrion Albert being beaten to death by his peers tell us about what kids are actually learning in schools? Far too often, dominant media, school administrators, politicians, and others insist on the pathology of privatized and collective violence that runs roughshod over kids' lives in and out of schools. In the case of the police officer who brutally beat Marshawn, the comforting solution is to privatize the assault, an example of an individual pathology, the work of a "bad apple." The beating of Derrion by other kids similarly speaks to an alleged culture of depravity that has been defined for the last three decades as black, urban, and dangerous. In both cases, the systemic neoliberal economic, institutional, educational, and racist underpinnings of such violence disappear into the logic of individual pathology or into the always crowd-pleasing categorization of the culture of blackness as pathological. Neither answer will do, at least not in an aspiring democracy. Finally, what do these acts of violence against children tell us about what kids are learning through the pedagogical force of the larger culture? What do they tell us about a society that refuses to recognize that the issue is not what is wrong with children, but what is wrong with American society?

NOTES

1. http://www.huffingtonpost.com/2009/10/07/marshawn-pitts-cop-caught_n_312354.html.
2. Mark Slouka, "Dehumanized: When Math and Science Rule the School," *Harper's Magazine* (September 2009), p. 34.
3. http://www.huffingtonpost.com/2009/09/27/beating-death-of-derrion_n_301319.html.

CHAPTER FOURTEEN

Tortured Memories and the Culture of War

For the last decade, we have lived through an historical period in which the United States surrendered its already tenuous claim to democracy. The frames through which democracy apprehends the lives of others as human beings worthy of respect, dignity, and human rights were sacrificed to a mode of politics and culture that simply became an extension of war, both at home and abroad. At home the punishing state increasingly replaced the welfare state, however ill-conceived, as more and more individuals and groups were treated as redundant, undeserving of those safety nets and basic protections that provide the conditions for living with a sense of security and dignity.[1]

Under such conditions, basic social supports were replaced by an increase in the production of prisons, the expansion of the criminal justice system into everyday life, and the further erosion of crucial civil liberties. Shared responsibilities gave way to shared fears, and the only distinction that seemed to resonate in the culture was between friends and patriots, on the one hand, and dissenters and enemies on the other.[2] State violence not only became acceptable, it was normalized as the government spied on its citizens, suspended the right of habeas corpus, sanctioned police brutality against those who questioned state power, relied on the state secrets privilege to hide its crimes, and increasingly reduced those public spheres that were designed to protect children to containment centers and warehouses that modeled themselves after prisons.

Fear both altered the landscape of democratic rights and values and dehuman-ized a population increasingly willing to look the other way as large segments of the population were dehumanized, incarcerated, or simply treated as disposable.[3] The dire consequences can be seen every day as the media reports a stream of tragic sto-ries about decent people losing their homes, more and more young people being incarcerated, and increasing numbers of people living in their cars, on the streets, or in tent cities. *The New York Times* offers up a frontpage story about young peo-ple leaving their recession-ridden families in order to live on the street, often sur-viving by selling their bodies for money.[4] Reports surface in the dominant media about unspeakable horrors being inflicted on children tortured in the "death cham-bers" of Iraq, Cuba, and Afghanistan.[5] And yet the American public barely blinks.

The Bush administration further eroded a culture inspired by democratic val-ues, replacing it with a culture of war. During the last decade, the language and ghostly shadow of war became all-embracing, not only eroding the distinction between war and peace, but putting into play a public pedagogy in which nearly every aspect of the culture was shaped by militarized knowledge, values, and ideals. From video games and Hollywood films aided by the Department of Defense to the ongoing militarization of public and higher education, the notion of the common good was subordinated to a military metaphysics, war-like values, and the dictates of the national security state.[6] War was no longer the last resort of a state intent on defending its territory. It morphed into a new form of public pedagogy—a type of cultural war machine—designed to shape and lead the society. War became the foundation for a politics that employed military language, concepts, and policing relations to address problems far beyond the familiar terrains of battle. In some cases, war was so aestheticized by the dominant media that it resembled an advertisement for a tourist industry. The upshot is that the meaning of war was rhetorically, visu-ally, and materially expanded to name, legitimate, and wage battles against social problems involving drugs, poverty, and our newfound enemy, Mexican immigrants.

As war became normalized as the central function of power and politics, it became a regular and normative element of American society, legitimated by a state of exception and emergency that became permanent rather than temporary. As the production of violence reached beyond traditionally defined enemies and threats, the state now took aim at terrorism, shifting its register of power by waging war on a concept, broadening its pursuits, tactics, and strategies against more than any spe-cific state, army, or location. The enemy was omnipresent, all the more difficult to root out and all the more convenient for expanding the tactics of surveillance, the culture of fear, and the resources of violence. War was now a commonplace feature of American domestic and foreign policy, as the country engaged in a battle that had no definitive end and demanded the constant use of violence.

It is difficult to imagine how any democracy could not be corrupted when war becomes the foundation of politics. Any democracy that makes war and state violence the organizing principle of society cannot survive for long, at least as a democratic entity. The country descended into a period in which society was increasingly organized through the production of both symbolic and material violence. A culture of cruelty emerged in the media, especially in the talk radio circuit, in which a sordid nationalism and a morally bankrupt nativism merged with a hyper-militarism and masculinity that scorned both reason and all those who fit into the stereotype of other, which appeared to include everyone who was not white and Christian. Dialogue, reason, and thoughtfulness slowly disappeared from the public realm as every encounter was framed within circles of certainty, staged as a fight to the death. As the civic and moral center of the country disappeared under the Bush administration, the language of the marketplace provided the only referent for understanding the obligations of citizenship and global responsibility, undeterred by a growing war machine and culture that produced jobs, goods, and furthered the war economy.

The war abroad entered a new phase with the release of the photos of detainees being tortured at Abu Ghraib prison. War as organized violence was stripped of its noble aims and delusional goal of promoting democracy and revealed state violence at its most degrading and dehumanizing moment. State power had become an instrument of torture, ripping into the flesh of human beings, raping women, and most abominably torturing children. Democracy had become a shell that not only defended the unthinkable but inflicted the most horrible mutilations on both adults and children deemed to be the enemies of democracy. But the mutilations were also inflicted against the body politic as politicians such as former Vice President Dick Cheney defended torture while the media addressed the question of torture not as a violation of democratic principles or human rights but as a strategy that may or may not produce concrete information. The utilitarian arguments used to defend a market-driven economy that only recognizes cost-benefit analyses had now reached their logical end point as similar arguments were now used to defend torture, even when it involved children. The pretense of democracy was stripped bare as it was revealed over and over again that the United States had become a torture state, aligning itself with infamous dictatorships such as those in Argentina and Chile during the 1970s. The United States government under the Bush administration had finally arrived at a point where the metaphysics of war, organized violence, and state terrorism prevented them from recognizing how much they were emulating the very acts of terrorism they claimed to be fighting. The circle had now been completed as the warfare state had been transformed into a torture state. Everything become permissible both at home and abroad just as the legal system, along with the market system, legitimated a punishing and ruthless mode of Economic Darwinism that viewed morality if not democracy itself as a weakness to be either scorned or ignored. Self-regulation now drove the market, and narrowly defined individual interests set the parameters of what was possible. The public collapsed into the private, and social responsibility was reduced to the arbitrary desires of the hermetic, asocial self. Not surprisingly, the inhuman and degrading not only entered public discourse and shaped the debate about war, state violence, and human rights abuses but served to legitimate such practices. Torture was normalized, and the promise of an aspiring democracy was irreparably damaged.

The United States under the Bush administration embarked on a war on terror that not only defended torture as a matter of official policy but furthered the conditions for the emergence of a culture of cruelty that profoundly altered the political and moral landscape of the country. As torture became normalized under the Bush administration, it not only corrupted American ideals and political culture, it also passed over to the dark side in sanctioning the unimaginable and unspeakable torture of children. While the rise of the torture state has been a subject of intense controversy, too little has been said by intellectuals, academics, artists, writers, parents, and politicians about how state violence under the Bush administration set in motion a public pedagogy and political culture that not only legitimated the systematic torture of children but did so with the complicity of a dominant media that either denied such practices or simply ignored them. The focus on children here is deliberate because young people provide a powerful referent for not only the long-term consequences of social policies, if not the future itself, but also because they offer a crucial index to measure the moral and democratic values of a nation. Children are the heartbeat of politics because they speak to the best of its possibilities and promises, and yet they have in the last few years become the vanishing point of moral debate, either irrelevant because of their age, discounted because they are largely viewed as commodities, or scorned because they are considered a threat to adult society.

I have written in *Youth in a Suspect Society* and in this book that how we educate our youth is connected to the collective future we hope for.[7] Actually, how we educate youth became meaningless as a moral issue under the Bush administration, because youth were not only devalued and considered unworthy of a decent life and future (one reason they were denied adequate health care), they were also reduced to the status of the inhuman and depraved and subjected to cruel acts of torture in sites that were as illegal as they were barbaric. In this instance, youth became the negation of not only politics but also the future itself. But more is at stake here than making such crimes visible. There is also the moral and political imperative of raising serious questions about the challenges the Obama administration must address in light of this shameful period in American history, especially if it wants to reverse such policies and make a claim to restoring any vestige of American democracy. Of course, when a country makes torture legal and extends the disciplinary mechanisms of pain, humiliation, and suffering to children, it suggests that far too many people looked away while this was happening and in doing so allowed conditions to emerge that made the unspeakable act of justifying the torture of children a matter of state policy. It is time for Americans to face up to these crimes and engage in a national dialogue about the political, economic, educational, and social conditions that allowed such a dark period to emerge in American history and to hold those responsible accountable for such acts.

The Obama administration is under fire for its embrace of many of Bush's policies, but what is most disturbing is its willingness to make war, secrecy, and the suspension of civil liberties a central feature of its own policies. Obama, in his desire to look ahead, recycles a dangerous form of historical and social amnesia and overlooks the political and civic pathology he inherited. Memory at its best is unsettling and sometimes even dangerous in its call for individuals to become moral and political witnesses, to take risks, to embrace history not merely as a critique, but as a warning about how fragile democracy is and what will likely happen when the principles, ideals, and elements of the culture that sustain it are allowed to slip away, overtaken by forces that embrace death rather than life, fear rather than hope, insularity rather than solidarity. Robert Hass, the American poet, has suggested that the job of education, its political job, "is to refresh the idea of justice going dead in us all the time." Justice is slipping away, once again, under the Obama administration, but it is not just the government's job to keep it from "going dead." It is also our job—as parents, citizens, individuals, and educators—not merely as a matter of social obligation or moral responsibility, but as an act of politics, agency, and possibility.

NOTES

1. Loïc Wacquant, *Punishing the Poor: The Neoliberal Government of Social Insecurity* (Durham, NC: Duke University Press, 2009).
2. See Zygmunt Bauman's critical analysis of Carl Schmitt's popularity regarding this distinction in his *Living on Borrowed Time* (London: Polity Press, 2010), especially "Conversation III."
3. Henry A. Giroux, *The Abandoned Generation: Beyond the Culture of Fear* (New York: Palgrave, 2004).
4. Ian Urbina, "Recession Drives Surge in Youth Runaways," *The New York Times* (October 25, 2009), p. A1.
5. Henry A. Giroux, *Hearts of Darkness: Torturing Children in the War on Terror* (Boulder, CO: Paradigm, 2010).
6. Nick Turse, *The Complex: How the Military Invades Our Everyday Lives* (New York: Metropolitan Books, 2008).
7. Henry A. Giroux, *Youth in a Suspect Society* (New York: Palgrave Macmillan, 2009).

CHAPTER FIFTEEN

Youth Beyond the Politics of Hope

The counter-revolution that has gripped the United States since the late 1980s has been somewhat modified with the election of Barack Obama to the presidency. Unfortunately the dark times that befell us under the second Bush administration have far from disappeared, especially for young people. The assault that the second Bush administration waged on practically every remnant of the public good—from the Constitution to the environment to public education—appears to have somewhat lessened its grip as the Obama regime moves into its second year in power. Yet the range, degree, and severity of the problems the Obama team has inherited from the Bush administration seem almost too daunting to address successfully: a war raging in two countries, a legacy of torture and secret prisons, a dismantling of the regulatory apparatus, a poisonous inequality that allocates resources to the rich and misery to the poor, an imperial presidency that shredded the balance of power, a looming ecological apocalypse, a ruined reputation abroad, and a financial crisis that is almost unprecedented in American history—policies and conditions that have brought great suffering to millions of Americans and many millions more throughout the world. But the crisis that is most often forgotten or repressed in the daily headlines of gloom is the war that is being waged at home, primarily against young people, who have historically been linked to the promise of a better life, one that they would both inherit and reproduce for future generations. In a radical free-market culture, when hope is precarious and bound to commodities and a corrupt financial system, young people are no longer at risk: they *are* the risk. Young people are no longer troubled: they *are* trouble.

The conditions produced by the financial crisis have resulted in the foreclosure of not only millions of family homes but also the future of young people, as the prospects of the unborn are mortgaged off in the interests of corporate power and profits. As wealth moved furiously upward into private hands for the last several decades,[1] any talk about the future has less to do with young people than with short-term investments, quick turnovers in profits, and the dismantling of the welfare state. Moreover, the destruction of the welfare state, or even better the social state, has gone hand-in-hand with the emergence of a prison-industrial complex and a new penal state that regulates, controls, contains, and punishes those who are not privileged by the benefits of class, color, immigration status, and gender. How else to explain a national prison population that has grown from 200,000 in 1973 to slightly over 2.3 million in 2010? It gets worse. The Bureau of Justice Statistics reports that at the end of 2007 "over 7.3 million people were on probation, in jail or prison, or on parole—3.2 percent of all U.S. adult residents or 1 in every 31 adults."[2]

As policing, containment, and imprisonment merge with the market-driven dictates of casino capitalism, the reasons for and redress of misfortune are now placed entirely in the hands of isolated individuals. As the circuitry of social control and power redefines the meaning of youth, particularly those marginalized by class and color, young people are subjected to a number of indiscriminate, cruel, and potentially illegal practices by the criminal justice system. In the age of instant credit and quick profits, human life is reduced to just another commodity to be bought and sold, and the logic of short-term investments undercuts long-term investments in public welfare, young people, and a democratic future. Not surprisingly, young people as a symbol of long-term commitment are now viewed as a liability rather than an asset. Barack Obama repeatedly insisted both before and after his election that the United States must live up to its obligations to future generations. While Obama has only been in office for a few years, it is becoming increasingly difficult to see how young people are benefitting from that promise. Obama's economic policies are being shaped by people who caused the crisis, thus condemning children to massive levels of unemployment and a future without hope. His education policies are simply an extension of the discredited Bush approach to schooling, and Arne Duncan, the secretary of education, appears unusually illiterate when it comes to being able to pose a democratic vision for education, given his love of the market, testing, and his dislike for any mode of knowledge and classroom pedagogy that cannot be measured. Duncan's policies turn the language of school reform into the discourse of punishment and extend the neoliberal, zombie-like war being waged against young people. For example, as Jesse Hagopian points out, the

Race to the Top Initiative is tied to a $4.3 billion fund to make states compete for desperately needed education money by using eligibility requirements to push for charter schools—schools publicly funded by taxpayers, yet run privately, outside the control of local school boards—and merit pay schemes where teachers are paid according to student test scores. Arne's turnaround play proposes closing some 5,000 schools across the country and firing entire teaching staffs at schools perceived to be failing.[3]

When Jesse Hagopian interviewed Duncan, he asked him why he is putting money into charter schools when a recent Stanford study suggested that public schools on the whole outperformed charter schools. Hagopian's point was that if public schools are outperforming charter schools, why not invest public money in schools that are accountable to public control? In response, Duncan provided what can only be viewed as a nonsensical answer: "There is nothing inherently good or bad about charters."[4]

Not only is this answer nonsensical, but it reveals the lack of compassion and understanding necessary to curb the kind of violence being waged against young people in public schools, on the streets, and in a range of other spheres. Clearly, the war against young people does not begin and end with public schooling. Equally important is the need to recognize that American society is still in a state of permanent war, and many young people, especially poor minorities, will continue to die or be maimed in imperial struggles abroad. We are still the largest arms dealer in the world, and we have a Republican Party whose only goal seems to be to block every policy Obama proposes regardless of whether it is good for the country as a whole. The winners in this logic are the militarists, the defense industries, the bankers, the most powerful corporations, the ruling elite, the advocates of ideological rigidity, and commanding financial institutions.

Under such conditions, there is a need to analyze the forces that ushered in such dark times and examine their most unlikely and often invisible victims—those young people who now symbolize trouble rather than promise, and who experience daily the repercussions of adult neglect, if not scorn, especially those youth for whom race and class loom large in their lives. This is a generation of young people who have been betrayed by the irresponsibility of their elders and relegated to the margins of society, often in ways that suggest that they are an excess, redundant, a drain on the empire of consumption—a population who, in the age of rampant greed and rabid individualism, appear to be largely expendable and disposable.

For many young people, these are dangerous times, and there is a need to develop a new language for addressing both the suffering many young people experience, albeit to different degrees, and the promise that an aspiring democracy might offer them. We seem to live at a time when politics is divorced from a sense of outrage as well as a sense of hope. In the face of a culture awash in consumerism, spectacularized hyper-violence, trash television, racist talk radio, and trivialized journalism, there seems to be little concern, if not understanding, of a number of forces—including an unfettered free-market ideology, a dehumanizing economic system, the rise of the racially skewed punishing state, and the attack on public and higher education—that have come together to pose a threat to young people and that are so extreme that they can be accurately described as a "war on youth."

Yet, in spite of such manufactured public indifference, it is imperative that educators, parents, and other concerned Americans do everything they can to make visible those forces responsible for the dire state of today's youth. Clearly, such an intervention must arise from the belief that individual and collective resistance is born out of awareness, critical education, discerning judgment, and an ethic of mutuality—all of which suggests a struggle that is as educational as it is political, with no line dividing one from the other. While there were good reasons to celebrate initially the Obama victory, what has become clear is that it never offered any guarantees that the political, economic, and social conditions that have brought us to the brink of disaster would fundamentally change. Substantive and lasting change must come from below: from young people, students, workers, intellectuals, artists, academics, parents, workers, labor unions, social movements, and other individuals and groups willing not just to demonstrate for equality, freedom, and social justice but to organize in order to push hope over the tipping point, push politics in a new democratic and socially just direction, and engage in a collective struggle that takes power away from political and corporate elites, returning it to the people who are the real source of any viable democracy.

As I have pointed out in much of my work, the changing punitive conditions youth now face in the new millennium and the degree to which they have been put at risk by reactionary social policies, institutional mismanagement, and shifting cultural attitudes has assumed the status of a low-intensity war. While youth have always represented an ambiguous category, they have within the last thirty years been under assault in ways that are entirely new, and they now face a world that is far more dangerous than at any other time in recent history. And these new conditions demand a new set of categories and vocabulary for understanding the changing problems youth face within the relentless expansion of a global market society, one that punishes all youth by treating them largely as commodities.

But if the commodification of American society represents a soft war on youth, the hard war takes a different and more extreme form and subjects poor youth and youth of color to the harshest elements, values, and dictates of a growing youth-crime complex, governing them through a logic of punishment, surveillance, and control. In this instance, even as the corporate state is in turmoil, it is transformed into a punishing state, and certain segments of the youth population become the object of a new mode of zombie-like governance based on the crudest forms of disciplinary control. For example, a recent study, *The Consequences of Dropping Out of High School*, published by Northeastern University, states that on any given day "1.4% of the nation's 16–24 year olds were institutionalized of whom nearly 93% were residing in correctional facilities (jails, prisons, juvenile detention centers)."[5] These figures become even more alarming when analyzed through the harsh realities of economic deprivation and racial disadvantage. Nearly one in every ten young male high school dropouts was either in jail or juvenile detention. And for African American youth, the figure jumps to one in four high school dropouts being incarcerated. There are over 6.2 million high school dropouts in the United States, and they lack both decent educational opportunities, adequate job-training programs, and the chance for decent employment. For instance, the jobless rate for young African American males has risen to a staggering 69 percent while for whites it is 54 percent. What becomes clear is that the high school dropout and unemployment rates are increasingly driving staggering incarceration rates for young people. As this recession unfolds, young people, especially poor minorities who fail to finish high school, bear the brunt of a system that leaves them uneducated and jobless, ultimately offering them one of the two bailouts available for populations largely considered disposable—either the juvenile detention center or prison. What does it say about a society that can put trillions of dollars into two useless wars, offer generous tax cuts for the rich, and bail out corrupt banks and insurance industries but cannot provide a decent education and job training opportunities for its most disadvantaged youth?

Out of ethical necessity, any discourse about youth should raise serious questions about the social and political responsibility of educators in addressing the plight of young people today. What is the purpose of higher education and its faculties in light of the current assault on young people, especially since it is education that provides the intellectual foundation and values for young people to understand, interrogate, and transform when necessary the world in which they live? Matters of popular consciousness, public sentiment, and individual and social agency are far too important as part of a larger political and educational struggle not be taken seriously by academics who advocate the long and difficult project of democratic reform. Tragically, few intellectuals providing critical commentary on the current conditions affecting youth offer any insights regarding how the educational force of the culture actually works pedagogically to reproduce dominant ideologies, values, identifications, and consent. How exactly is it possible to imagine a more just, more equitable transformation in government and economics without a simultaneous transformation in culture, consciousness, social identities, and values? Finally, it is impossible to understand the current crisis of youth and democracy without situating such a crisis in a larger theoretical and historical context.

In addressing this challenge, it is important to provide a broader analysis of what can be called the politics of free-market fundamentalism and disposability, examining it as an educational, cultural, and political discourse that has gutted the notion of the social state and produced a set of policies that lay the groundwork for a politics of greed and disposability that has had and continues to have dire consequences for society at large, and especially for young people. As home foreclosures reach into the millions, as more than fifteen million workers join the ranks of the unemployed, as the ranks of the homeless expand beyond the wildest predictions, children bear the brunt of these problems. As I have mentioned in previous chapters, the notion of the child as symbol of adult responsibility and the hopeful future once symbolized by the figure of the child are disappearing from American life. Children now worry about how they can help their parents get a job, make a mortgage payment, and simply afford to get food for a meal.

We now live in a country in which the pervasive and all-embracing reach of a reactionary, racist, and greed-driven politics has reached its endpoint and reveals its own arrogance and cruelty every day in the suffering of those individuals, children, and families shipwrecked by the recklessness of a society that only believes in short-term investments and the smell of fast profits. In response to this type of barbaric behavior and systemic misuse of power, the American public is further insulted by a culture of cruelty that is offered up by right-wing media pundits as a form of cheap theater. Fortunately, power is never completely on the side of domination, nor is it entirely in the hands of those who view youth as an excess to be contained or burden to be expelled. Power is also born of a realistic sense of hope, one that situates new possibilities and dreams of the future within the realities of current structures of domination and oppression. Young people deserve more, and it is up to those who are willing to assume a measure of civic courage and social responsibility to come together and say enough is enough, and then mobilize to force Obama to take seriously what it might mean to live up to the principles of both an aspiring democracy and, yes, the Nobel Peace Prize. But more importantly, young people and others need to develop social movements that create a political party that refuses the center-right politics of the Democratic and Republican parties. This would be a party that matches its ideals and rhetoric with action and policies that benefit working- and middle-class people and not simply the elite running the financial institutions; this would be a politics that provides universal health care, expands social protections for the disadvantaged, and democraticizes wealth and power in the United States so as to give real meaning to a democratic politics. Zombie politics feeds off the lawlessness caused by massive inequalities in wealth, income, and power. It's time to bury the dead and let the living once again inhabit the regions of government, the media, the economy, and other crucial spheres of power.

Notes

1. See, for example, "Dollars and Sense and United for a Fair Economy", *The Wealth Inequality Reader*, 2nd ed. (Boston: Dollars and Sense, 2008); See especially, Michael Schwalbe, *Rigging the Game: How Inequality Is Reproduced in Everyday Life* (New York: Oxford University Press, 2008); Richard Wilkinson and Kate Pickett, *The Spirit Level: Why Greater Equality Makes Societies Stronger* (New York: Bloomsbury Press, 2009).
2. U.S. Department of Justice, "Bureau of Justice Statistics," accessed January 2008, http://www.ojp.usdoj.gov/bjs/pandp.htm.
3. Jesse Hagopian, "Schooling Arne Duncan," CommonDreams.Org (July 21, 2010). www.commondreams.org/pring/58538
4. Ibid.
5. Andrew Sum, et al., *The Consequences of Dropping Out of High School* (Boston: Center for Labor Market Studies, Northeastern University, October 2009), http://www.clms.neu.edu/publication/documents/The_Consequences_of_Dropping_Out_of_High_School.pdf

SECTION IV

Conclusion

CHAPTER SIXTEEN

Winter in America

Democracy Gone Rogue

The absolute. . .spells doom to everyone when it is introduced into the political realm.
HANNAH ARENDT [1]

Democracy in the United States is experiencing both a crisis of meaning and a legitimation crisis. As the promise of an aspiring democracy is sacrificed more and more to corporate and military interests, public spheres have largely been commercialized, and democratic practices have been reduced to market relations, stripped of their worth, and subject to the narrow logics of commodification and profit-making. Empowerment has little to do with providing people with the knowledge, skills, and power to shape the forces and institutions that bear down on their lives and is now largely defined under the rubric of being a savvy consumer. When not equated with free-market capitalism, democracy is reduced to the empty rituals of elections largely shaped by corporate money and indifferent to relations of power that make a mockery out of equality, democratic participation, and collective deliberation.

The undoing of democracy as a substantive ideal is most visible in the illegal legalities perpetuated by the Bush/Cheney regime and reproduced under the presidency of Barack Obama that extend from the use of military commissions, the policy of indefinite detention, suppressing evidence of torture, maintaining secret and illegal prisons in Afghanistan, to the refusal to prosecute former high-level government officials who sanctioned acts of torture and other violations of human rights.

As part of the crisis of legitimation, democracy's undoing can be seen in the anti-democratic nature of governance that has increasingly shaped domestic and foreign policy in the United States, policies that have been well documented by a number of writers extending from Noam Chomsky to Chris Hedges. What is often missed, however, is how such anti-democratic forces work at home in ways that are less visible and—when they are visible—seem to become easily normalized, removed from any criticism as they settle into that ideological fog called common sense.

If the first rule of politics is to make power invisible, the second rule is to devalue critical thought by relieving people of the necessity to think critically and hold power accountable—always in the name of common sense. Under the populist rubric of common sense, democracy is now used to invoke rationalizations for invading other countries, bailing out the rich, and sanctioning the emergence of a national security state that increasingly criminalizes the social relations and behaviors that characterize those most excluded from what might be called the consumer and celebrity-laden dreamworlds of a market-driven society. As democracy is removed from relations of equality, justice, and freedom, it undergoes a legitimation crisis as it is transformed from a mode of politics that subverts authoritarian tendencies to one that reproduces them. Used to gift wrapping the interests and values of an authoritarian culture, the rhetoric of democracy is now invoked to legitimate its opposite, a discourse of security and a culture of fear enlisted by intellectuals, pundits, and other anti-public intellectuals as all-embracing registers for mobilizing a rampant nationalism, hatred of immigrants, and a bunker politics organized around an "us-versus-them" mentality. When tied to the discourse of democracy, such practices seem beyond criticism, part of a center-right mentality that views such policies as natural and God-given—beyond ethical and political reproach.

As the country undermines its own democratic values, violence and anti-democratic practices become institutionalized throughout American culture, their aftershocks barely noticed, testifying to how commonplace they have become. For instance, as one major report indicated recently, more "than 60 percent of children were exposed to violence within the past year . . . [with] nearly half of adolescents surveyed . . . assaulted at least once in the previous year [and] one-quarter had witnessed an act of violence."[2] In just one week, the media reported on a 12-year-old student who was arrested for doodling on her desk at school. Her teacher thought it was a criminal act and called the New York City police who promptly handcuffed her and took her to the local police station.[3] In Montgomery, Maryland, a 13-year-old student at Roberto Clemente Middle School was taken out of class by security officers after she refused to recite the Pledge of Allegiance.[4] The mainstream media provide glimpses of such assaults but rarely are they analyzed within a broader political and social context that highlights the political and economic conditions that make them possible. For instance, such assaults say nothing about the increasing militarization of public schools, the right-wing attempts to defund them so they can be privatized, the rampant inequality that approximates a form of class warfare, or the racism often at the heart of such practices.[5]

Such actions are now normalized within the discourse of an authoritarian politics fueled by both the increasing militarization of all levels of society and legitimated further through a harsh and cruel notion of Economic Darwinism. There are no shades of gray in this militarized discourse, no room for uncertainty, thoughtfulness, or dialogue, since this view of engagement is modeled on notions of war, battle, winning at all costs, and eliminating the enemy. How this discourse plays out in shaping public education is particularly revealing. Complex understanding is banished under the call for a thoughtless, one-size-fits-all, zero tolerance policy in schools; intelligence is now quantified using formulas that may be useful for measuring the heights of trees but little else; and teachers are deskilled through the widespread adoption of both a governing-through-crime pedagogy and an equally debilitating pedagogy of high-stakes testing.

Resentment builds as social services either collapse or are stretched to the limit at a time when over 15 million people are unemployed and over "91.6 million people—more than 30 percent of the entire population—fell below 200 percent of the federal poverty line."[6] Emerging out of this void and shaping a more militaristic anti-politics are the anti-public intellectuals and their corporate sponsors, eager to fill the air with populist anger by supporting right-wing groups, Sarah Palin types, Glenn Beck clones, and self-styled patriots who bear an eerie resemblance to the beliefs and violent politics of the late Timothy McVeigh, who bombed a federal building in Oklahoma City in 1995.[7]

This emerging conglomerate and diverse group of anti-public intellectuals, political pundits, and populist agitators express a deep-seated hatred for government (often labeled as either socialist or fascist), progressive politics, and the notion that everyone should have access to a quality education, decent health care, employment, and other public services. Under such circumstances, it is not surprising that Sarah Palin, in addressing the recent National Tea Party convention, stated: "I will live, I will die for the people of America, whatever I can do to help."[8] Surely, these words leave little ambiguity for members of the John Birch Society, right-wing militia groups, Oath Keepers white supremacists, and other armed anti-government groups that appear to be growing in numbers and influence under the Obama presidency. But while these lines received much attention from the dominant media, the more telling comment took place when Palin offered the Tea Party audience lines she lifted from one of the more fascistic films released by Hollywood in the last decade, *Fight Club*. Inhabiting the character of a self-styled, pathologically violent maverick, Tyler Durden (played by Brad Pitt), whose misogyny is matched by his willingness to engage in acts of militia-inspired terrorism, Palin unabashedly mimics one of Tyler's now-famous wisecracks in attacking Obama's clever rhetoric with the line, "How's that hopey, changey stuff working out for ya?"⁹ Going rogue in this context suggests more than a compensatory quip for any kind of sustained analysis; instead it offers a seductive populist reference to lawless violence.

This somewhat confused but reckless appropriation of the discourse of glamorized violence suggests the not-so-subtle ways in which violence has become the framing mechanism for engaging in almost any mode of politics. Under such circumstances, politics shares an ignoble connection to a kind of soft terrorism, a kind of symbolic violence blatantly tied to the pathologies of corporate corruption, state-sanctioned brutality, and authoritarian modes of engagement. As violence and politics merge, the militarization, disciplining, and oppressive regulation of American society continue, often legitimated by a popular culture in which the spectacles of celebrity idiocy and violence become the only stimuli left to shock people out of their boredom or offer them an outlet for their anger. But it continues in ways that seem incidental rather than connected, diffused of its real meaning and abstracted from the politics that informs it—hence, it slips into a kind of invisibility, wrapped in the logic of common sense. Under its common sense rubric, homelessness and poverty are now criminalized; schools are dominated by zero tolerance policies that turn public schools into a low-intensity war zone; school lock-downs are the new fire drills; the welfare state morphs into the warfare state, and university research is increasingly funded by the military and designed for military and surveillance purposes. In one of the more frightening examples of the militarization of American society, David Price has brilliantly documented how government intelligence agencies are now placing "unidentified students with undisclosed links to intelligence agencies into university classrooms . . . and has gone further . . . than any previous intelligence initiative since World War Two. Yet, the program spreads with little public notice, media coverage, or coordinated multicampus resistance."¹⁰

Is it any wonder that when intellectuals in the social sciences and medical fields assist in the illegal torture of "enemy combatants" or embed themselves in military-sponsored counter-insurgency campaigns, such practices rarely get the critical attention they deserve? All too often, the blathering disciples of common sense tell us that politics is rooted in natural laws, unhampered by critical thought—a kind of plain folk wisdom. Such appeals to the alleged obvious suggest that thinking is at odds with politics, and its hidden order of politics is hateful of those public spaces where speaking and acting human beings actually engage in critical dialogue, exercise discriminating judgments, and address important social problems. Common sense is in effect an anti-politics because it removes questions of agency, governance, and critical thought from politics itself.

As part of the logic of plain speak, scapegoating rhetoric replaces the civic imagination, and a brutalizing, calculating culture of fear, demonization, and criminalization replaces judgment, emptying politics of all substantive meaning. In this discourse, there are no social problems, only individual failings. Poverty, inadequate health care, soaring public debt, the bailout of corrupt financial institutions, the prison binge, and the destruction of public and higher education cannot be addressed by the logic of common sense, because such issues point to broad, complex considerations that demand a certain amount of understanding, literacy, and a sense of political and moral responsibility—all enemies of the anti-public intellectuals who wrap themselves in the populist appeal of a know-nothing common sense. The populist appeal to the so-called obvious makes human beings superfluous, depoliticizes politics, and transforms human beings into the living dead, unable to recognize "that politics requires judgment, artful diplomacy, and judicious discrimination."[11] Common sense occupies the antithesis of Hannah Arendt's insistence that debate constitutes the very essence of political life."[12] This is the central message of the zombie-like Fox News, Sean Hannity, and other right-wing fundamentalists who live in circles of certainty and reject any real attempt at debate, persuasion, and deliberation as the essence of politics. Their populist appeal to common sense to justify their various views of the world rejects both enlarged ways of thinking, thoughtfulness, and the exercise of critical judgment. Such a discourse creates a zombie politics in which deliberation is blocked and the ethos of democracy is stripped of any meaning.

A zombie politics enmeshed in the production of organized violence, surveillance, market-driven corruption, and control, buttressed by an appeal to common sense, blocks the path to open inquiry. War not only becomes normalized under such circumstances, it becomes a defining force in shaping all aspects of society, including its use of science and technology. Put differently, as warlike values become more prevalent in American society, science and technology are increasingly being harnessed in the interest of militarized and commercialized values and applications. For example, the defense industries are developing drone aircraft that can be used to deliver high-tech violence not only abroad but also at home. Unmanned drones, fitted with surveillance cameras, will soon be used to monitor demonstrations. As the technology becomes more advanced, the drones will be mounted with taser guns, rubber bullets, and other non-lethal weaponry in order to contain allegedly unruly individuals and crowds.[13] High-tech weapons have already been used on American protesters, and as the state relies more and more on military values, money, and influence to shape its most basic institutions, the use of organized violence against civilians will become more commonplace. For instance, at the 2009 G20 summit of world leaders, democracy took a hit as the Pittsburgh police used sonic cannons against protestors.[14] These high-tech weapons were used previously by the U.S. military against Somali pirates and Iraqi insurgents and create sounds loud enough to damage eardrums and potentially produce fatal aneurysms. In public schools, surveillance has become so widespread that one school in Rosemont, Pennsylvania, issued over 1,800 laptops to high school students and then used the webcams fitted on the computers to spy on them. The mainstream media hardly blinked, while the public yawned.

Common sense may be good or bad in terms of its value, but in all cases it is unreflective sense and as such short-cuts the types of critical inquiry fundamental to an engaged public and an aspiring society. But it is particularly dangerous when it becomes the pedagogical message of choice for much of the conservative-driven media. Surely, common sense is of little help in explaining the existence of brain research that is now being used to understand and influence how people respond to diverse sales and political pitches. Nor does it explain why there is not a huge public outcry over the emergence of a field such as neuromarketing, designed by politicians and corporations who are "using MRIs, EEGs, and other brain-scan and medical technology to craft irresistible media messages designed to shift buying habits, political beliefs and voting patterns."[15] Nor does it explain the politics or the lack of public resistance to food industries using the new media to market junk food to children. Zombie politics loves to depoliticize any vestige of individual agency and will. How else to explain a story by *New York Times* writer Nicholas D. Kristof, that legitimates the notion that political judgments are primarily the result of how our brains are hard wired. This is the ultimate expression of anti-politics in which matters of agency are now removed from any sense of responsibility, relegated to the brave new world of genetic determinism.

Under such circumstances, memory is lost; history is erased; knowledge becomes militarized, and education becomes more of a tool of domination than of empowerment. One result is not merely a collective ignorance over the meaning, nature, and possibilities of politics but a disdain for democracy itself that provides the condition for a lethal combination of political apathy and cynicism on the one hand and a populist anger and an ethical hardening of the culture on the other. Symbolic and real violence are now the defining features of American society. Instead of appealing to the principles of social justice, moral responsibility, and civic courage, the anti-public intellectuals and the market-driven institutions that support them laud common sense. What they don't mention is that underlying such appeals is a hatred not merely for government but for democracy itself. The rage will continue and the flirtations with violence will mount. Going rogue is now a metaphor for the death of democratic values and support for modes of symbolic and potentially real violence in which all vestiges of thought, self-reflection, and dialogue are destroyed.

As I have pointed out throughout this book, while the presence of zombies seems to dominate the news and the American political and cultural landscape, it does not signal the end of democratic politics. In fact, the increasing presence of the hyper-dead makes the need for resistance to such a politics all the more obvious, especially regarding those public spheres and institutions that produce knowledge, ideas, desires, and values crucial to an aspiring democracy. While the struggle for reclaiming the government as a responsible social state capable of both placing limits on capital and providing protections for all Americans has to be central to such a challenge, so does the struggle over culture as a form of public pedagogy. The likes of Beck, Limbaugh, and Palin matter not simply because of what they say, but because of the emergence and influence of anti-democratic institutions and the formations of capital that support them.

Power does not work simply through the control and influence of wealth, income, and resources. It also has to legitimate itself, and for that it needs to create a pedagogical culture through which it can promote its ideologies and values. Vast right-wing cultural apparatuses now exist in the mainstream media, on college campuses, and in the government—a kind of stealth pedagogical machine that does everything it can to promote its political agenda. The current fiasco in Texas and Arizona speaks to the seriousness of such a struggle as ethnic studies are banned, social studies curricula are rewritten so as to erase any vestige of progressive history, and freedom is sabotaged as it is abstracted from politics and reduced to the practice of consumerism. Mythic history now combines with a notion of freedom that is as reactionary as it is depoliticizing. Zombie politics thrives on a culture of blinding illiteracy, and for such a culture to be challenged, labor, youth, unions, and other groups must unite over the need to address at the very least two pressing and interrelated issues.

Effective resistance to zombie politics first requires addressing the political, economic, and cultural conditions of massive inequality produced by casino capitalism. These conditions must be challenged in every sphere in which such injustices appear. Such inequality is destructive of human lives and human societies, defines matters of life and death—whose life is valued and whose life only counts as redundant and disposable—and determines which members of society will have access to vital resources and which ones won't.[16] This is demonstrated by the inequitable funding of public schools and political campaigns, the poisonous influence of corporate lobbyists in shaping legislation that benefits corporations and the rich, access to quality health care based on wealth rather than need, and the massive corrupt financial institutions that make a mockery of democracy while providing a beachhead for expanding inequality in every aspect of our lives.

The second most pressing issue involves the educational force of political and popular culture. Democratic ideas cannot exist without the public spheres that make them possible. Culture in the form of the Internet and mass media is the most powerful influence now used by the hyper-dead to promote their zombie politics. These spheres must be recovered. Intellectuals, parents, unions, workers, and other concerned citizens need to reclaim those places that give the voiceless a voice, allow those marginalized by class and race to speak, and offer everyone the opportunity to reclaim an America that currently offers them little hope in terms of a better and more just life. This not only means using alternative media to counter the hate-mongers, the conservative foundations, and right-wing radio and television, but also organizing in churches, synagogues, mosques, union halls, and public schools in order to collectively reclaim such institutions as democratic public spheres while gaining the experience needed to challenge zombie pedagogy in all of its manifestations throughout the culture and society.

Hannah Arendt has written that there are turning points in history when "the decline of the old, the birth of the new, is not necessarily an affair of continuity." What emerges in this liminal space between generations, according to Arendt, is a "kind of historical no man's land" that can only be described in terms of "no longer and not yet."[17] Today, we are living in one of these in-between times. The looming abyss is most obvious between the "no longer" of casino capitalism and the politics of the hyper-dead and the "not yet," which holds the potential of a new politics to emerge and assert the imperatives of a democracy that values trust, compassion, equality, freedom, and social justice. As Americans, we must choose now whether to fall back into a pit of despair and death, ever widening to contain all but the immensely rich and powerful, or to move forward as politicized individuals and organized communities into a future rooted in and sustained by democratic principles. The "not yet" of this presently unknown future demands of us that we connect thoughtful critique and outrage to a notion of realizable hope and that we heed a rallying cry for justice against a zombie politics in which democracy has been reduced to a graveyard for the hyper-dead. Hopefully, the voices of reason and justice will recognize how serious this threat to democracy really is, and when they do, they will surely understand what Gil Scott-Heron meant when he talked about winter in America.

NOTES

1. Hannah Arendt, *On Revolution* (New York: Viking, 1963), p. 79.
2. Editorial, "Violence in the Lives of Children and Youth," *The Child Indicator* 10:1 (Winter 2010), p. 1.
3. Jenna Johnson, "Pledge of Allegiance Dispute Results in Md. Teacher Having to Apologize,"*The Washington Post* (February 24, 2010), p. B01.
4. Liliana Segura, "Arrested for Doodling on a Desk? 'Zero Tolerance' at Schools Is Going Way Too Far," *AlterNet* (February 27, 2010), http://www.alternet.org/rights/145834/arrested_for _doodling_on_a_desk_%22zero_tolerance%22_at_schools_is_going_way_too_far?page=entire.
5. I have taken this issue up in great detail in my *Youth in a Suspect Society: Democracy or Disposability?* (New York: Palgrave Macmillan, 2009).
6. Bob Herbert, "They Still Don't Get It," *The New York Times* (January 23, 2010), p. A21.

7. Frank Rich, "The Axis of the Obsessed and the Deranged," *The New York Times* (February 28, 2010), p. WK10.

8. Ibid.

9. Cited in Kathleen Hennessy, "Sarah Palin to Tea Party Convention: 'This is about the people,'" *Los Angeles Times* (February 7, 2010), http://articles.latimes.com/2010/feb/07/nation/la-na-tea-party7–2010feb07.

10. David Price, "How the CIA Is Welcoming Itself Back onto American University Campuses," *CounterPunch* 17:2 (January 16–31, 2010), p. 1.

11. Richard J. Bernstein, *The Abuse of Evil: The Corruption of Politics and Religion since 9/11* (Malden, MA: Polity Press, 2005) pp. 1–124.

12. Hannah Arendt, *Between Past and Future* (New York: Penguin Books, 1977), p. 72.

13. Paul Joseph Watson, "Surveillance Drones to Zap protesters into Submission," *Prison Planet* (February 12, 2010), http://www.prisonplanet.com/surveillance-drones-to-zap-protesters-into-submission.html. For an excellent source on how the robotic revolution is being used to transform the nature of war, see P.W. Singer, *Wired for War: The Robotic Revolution and Conflict in the 21st Century* (New York: Penguin Press, 2009).

14. News Blog, "G20 Protesters Blasted by Sonic Cannon," *The Guardian* (September 25, 2009), http://www.guardian.co.uk/world/blog/2009/sep/25/sonic-cannon-g20-pittsburgh. See also Ian Urbina, "Protesters Are Met by Tear Gas at G-20," *The New York Times* (September 25, 2009), p. A10.

15. See, for example, Rinaldo Brutoco and Madeleine Austin, "'Spellcasters': The Hunt for the 'Buy Button' in Your Brain," *TruthOut* (January 10, 2010), http://www.truthout.org/spellcasters-the-hunt-buy-button-your-brain56278?print.

16. Göran Therborn, "The Killing Fields of Inequality," *Open Democracy* (April 6, 2009), http://www.opendemocracy.net/article/the-killing-fields-of-inequality.

17. Hannah Arendt, "No Longer and Not Yet," in *Reflections on Literature and Culture*, ed. Susannah Yong-ah Gottlieb (Stanford: Stanford University Press, 2007), p. 121.

Index

Toby Miller
General Editor

Popular Culture and Everyday Life (PC&EL) is the new space for critical books in cultural studies. The series innovates by stressing multiple theoretical, political, and methodological approaches to commodity culture and lived experience, borrowing from sociological, anthropological, and textual disciplines. Each PC&EL volume develops a critical understanding of a key topic in the area through a combination of a thorough literature review, original research, and a student-reader orientation. The series includes three types of books: single-authored monographs, readers of existing classic essays, and new companion volumes of papers on central topics. Likely fields covered are: fashion; sport; shopping; therapy; religion; food and drink; youth; music; cultural policy; popular literature; performance; education; queer theory; race; gender; class.

For additional information about this series or for the submission of manuscripts, please contact:

Toby Miller
Department of Media & Cultural Studies
Interdisciplinary Studies Building
University of California, Riverside
Riverside, CA 92521

To order other books in this series, please contact our Customer Service Department:

(800) 770-LANG (within the U.S.)
(212) 647-7706 (outside the U.S.)
(212) 647-7707 FAX

Or browse online by series: www.peterlang.com